MAKE YOUR CHILD A LIFELONG READER

MAKE YOUR CHILD
A LIFELONG READER

*A Parent-Guided Program for Children
of All Ages Who Can't, Won't, or
Haven't Yet Started to Read*

Jacquelyn Gross, Ed.D.

in collaboration with Leonard Gross

JEREMY P. TARCHER, INC.
Los Angeles
Distributed by St. Martin's Press
New York

Library of Congress Cataloging in Publication Data

Gross, Jacquelyn, 1927-
  Make your child a lifelong reader.

  Bibliography: p.
  Includes index.
  1. Children—Books and reading. 2. Youth—Books and
reading. 3. Reading. I. Gross, Leonard. II. Title.
Z1037.A1G74 1986   028.5'3   85-27807
ISBN 0-87477-367-9

Jeremy P. Tarcher, Inc.
9110 Sunset Blvd.
Los Angeles, CA 90069

Design by Thom Dower

Manufactured in the United States of America
10 9 8 7 6 5 4 3 2 1

First Edition

For Linden and Jeff.

Acknowledgments

Leonard Gross, my husband, for his belief in this project and for his professional assistance.

Linden Gross, my daughter, for helping with the research and for writing "The Story of Sarah."

Contents

There is no Frigate like a Book
To take us lands away
Nor any Coursers like a Page
Of prancing Poetry—
This Traverse may the poorest take
Without oppress of Toll—
How frugal is the Chariot
That bears the Human Soul!
—Emily Dickinson

To the Parent

In all likelihood you have opened this book for at least one of three reasons:

You have a very young child who has not yet begun to read but will soon be starting school.

You have a child who has been through several years of schooling but can scarcely read.

You have a child who has learned to read adequately, but either won't read or shows virtually no interest in doing so.

In all three cases, the single person best qualified to help your child is yourself. No matter who you are, no matter what your educational background, if you can read this sentence, you can help your child become a reader.

For your child the payoff will begin at once and last a lifetime.

Children who become readers almost invariably become good students, if only because they have an easier time with schoolwork. More often than not, this easy access to learning stimulates curiosity just as surely as the smell of hamburgers cooking stimulates the appetite. The more interested children become, the more they read; the more they read, the better readers they become—and the more they learn about their world, their culture, themselves, and the variety of skills and special knowledge they will need to lead effective lives. The special dividend of this self-perpetuating process is the enhancement of powers of logic, which increase in direct proportion to the degree the mind is used, in the same way that muscles enlarge through exercise.

Only those children who become good readers go on to become *lifelong* readers as well, people who use books as resources and companions, and for enrichment, adventure, entertainment, and solace. "Every man who knows how to read has the power to magnify himself, to multiply the ways in which he exists, to make his life full, significant, and interesting," Aldous Huxley has written. No lifelong reader would argue with that statement, and for the parent, the implications are clear.

The greatest gift you can bestow upon your child is the assurance of your love. The second greatest gift you can give him or her is a set of intellectual tools with which to experience life in the most rewarding way possible. Reading is the most indispensable tool in that set; without it, no one can learn to use the others. No parent who loves a child can afford to let that child grow up either unable or unwilling to read.

It has always been a fundamental assumption of our society that we parents would provide food and shelter for our children, and the schools would teach them to read. As matters stand today, however, that assumption is no longer realistic. To the contrary, the evidence powerfully suggests that most of the children in America's schools today will not become lifelong readers and—to use the most conservative estimate justified by the data—one out of four of them will scarcely learn to read at all.

Our nation is producing illiterates and semiliterates at a rate that is frightening for us all—both as parents and as citizens. Newspaper and magazine stories about the problem generally put the number of illiterates in the United States at twenty-seven million, but Jonathan Kozol, the author of *Illiterate America* and the man most publicly associated with the problem, believes that this figure tells less than half the story. More than sixty million adults, he estimates, "cannot read enough to understand the poison warnings on a can of pesticide or the antidote instructions on a can of kitchen lye; nor can they understand the warnings of the sedative effects of non-prescription drugs, handle a checking account, read editorials in a newspaper, nor read the publications of the United States Census, which persists in telling us with stubborn, jingoistic pride that 99.4 percent of all Americans can read and write."

Each year, the number of illiterates in the United States increases by two and one-half million. Slightly more than half of this number are immigrants. The rest—more than one million each year—are products of our schools.

Statistics over the last half dozen years tell the same dismaying story. A study of the high school class of 1981 made by the National Center for Education showed that 27 percent of those children who had made it to the fifth grade did not go on to graduate. In my state, California, 31 percent of the class of 1982 dropped out of school before graduation, according to official figures. In large urban centers, the dropout rates are astronomical. In Los Angeles more than 44 percent of the students who entered high school failed to finish with the class of 1984. In New York City, the dropout rate was 45 percent. In Chicago that same year, 53 percent of the students had fallen by the wayside by the time their class was to graduate.

What accounts for this calamitous record?

When failure occurs in primary and secondary education, it is the inability to read with understanding and pleasure that is almost invariably at the heart of the problem. Asked by a *Los Angeles Times* education writer to account for the high level of failure in the city's school system, many of the teachers interviewed cited low-level reading ability as the major factor.

And the problem is not just the dropouts. Even those students who manage to make it through high school are plagued by reading deficiencies. To take just one example— Chicago—40 percent of the graduating seniors in the class of 1984 were reading at, or below, the junior high school level, and only 6,000 of the original class of 39,500 students were able to read at the twelfth-grade level.

How many American schoolchildren are having trouble learning to read? In the absence of official statistics, I attempted to answer this question myself by analyzing the percentages of children enrolled in remedial reading, minimum competency, compensatory, and special education programs. The result: well over half the children in our nation's schools are assigned to categories that, in one way or another, describe them as deficient readers.

Given this devastating evidence, the conclusion is inescapable that our schools are not doing the job we have entrusted to them. Children are not learning to read in acceptable numbers—and even the children who do learn are not reading as well as they could. *Why?*

As a concerned parent, you are undoubtedly as familiar as I am with the many explanations that have been offered: that many of the dropouts are from underprivileged homes in which there is no tradition of learning; that there has been a general drop in standards in the schools; that teachers today are not well trained and don't do an adequate job; that teaching is made more difficult by a lack of discipline in the schools; that children spend their time watching television when they should be cracking the books.

All of these arguments, which influence education generally, are applicable to reading problems, and all undoubtedly have some merit. As a teacher and an educator with a specialty in reading, I would like to add a theory of my own that has found support among many of my colleagues. In doing so, I do not mean to shoot off yet another cannon in the raging war over what's wrong with America's schools. My objective is to help you as a parent understand some of the obstacles to the acquisition of reading skills your child is encountering in the classroom. Once you understand that, you will also understand why it is imperative that you take the lead in helping your child become a lifelong reader. It is not exaggeration to suggest that, as matters stand today, it won't happen without you.

I believe that the reading problems in our schools today —and, indeed, the related learning problems—are the direct consequence of a relatively new and universally utilized system of reading instruction that simply doesn't work. Here, briefly, is how and why this system came into being.

It all began with Sputnik, a silvery artificial satellite the size of a softball launched into outer space by the Soviet Union in 1957. A wave of concern swept through the United States. To a nation that prided itself on its scientific ingenuity and industrial might, it was galling that the Russians, not the Americans, had been the first to put a man-made object into space. Because we were locked in a Cold War with the Russians, Sputnik was perceived both as a propaganda defeat and a strategic setback. As a means of regaining technological supremacy over the Soviet Union and restoring our tarnished prestige abroad, the government immediately instituted an all-out effort to support and improve education, primarily in science and technology. But to learn science and technology well required reading prowess—and so it was that the U.S. government determined to institute a new era of literacy. It would do so by funneling billions of dollars into the nation's educational program.

For the schools it was a windfall. Prior to Sputnik government support for education had been less than $400 million annually. Within fifteen years, the government's annual contribution would surpass $15 billion—nearly a 2,000 percent increase, even accounting for inflation.

But there was a kicker in the arrangement. Along with governmental support came governmental insistence on *accountability*. In effect, the government said to the schools, "We will give you money, but in order to continue to receive it, you must show us by the kinds of proofs we recognize that you are creating the kinds of people we need in order to win the Cold War. We want to know what we are getting for our money."

With the introduction of this accountability, education underwent a crucial shift in objectives and emphasis, a shift that would entirely change the manner in which children were taught.

Until then, education had maintained what might be called a "child-oriented" approach to teaching—that is, almost everything that took place in the classroom was geared to the child's interests, on the theory that learning occurred best when the learning activities were relevant to the child's life and promoted the child's goals. This approach bore the stamp of the most influential educator of his era, John Dewey, and it bore a label—"progressive education"—that served as a lightning rod during the political storms of the 1950s, in which anything progressive was suspected of being Communist inspired. These ideas, as formulated by the Progressive Education Association, among others, will scarcely sound seditious to today's generation of parents: it was thought that there should be opportunity in the schools for initiative and self-expression; group consciousness should be developed through participation in the school as a community; the curriculum should be based on the nature and needs of childhood; knowledge should be acquired through observation, investigation, experiment, and independent search for material; the teacher should guide the pupil in observing, experimenting, and forming judgments.

But how can one *measure* precisely what children have learned and how much more they know than they did before a learning experience transpired? One can see it and hear it, but not quantify it. If it can't be quantified, it can't be tested —which meant, post Sputnik, that the child-oriented approach to teaching would simply not produce the "proofs" the government demanded in its accountability approach to education.

An all-new, "testable" system was required.

Not only did the model for this system exist, it had already proved itself. It had been developed during World War II to teach recruits how to use and maintain military equipment and to develop whatever other skills they required to perform their military duties. This training plan was based on a time-tested industrial proposition, namely, if you simplify the tasks required of each worker, you reduce the need for high levels of skill.

It was strictly assembly-line thinking—it was not meant to be creative or spontaneous, just learned. As in assembly lines, the armed forces learning system required that all complex operations be broken down into a series of tiny, discrete steps—steps so simple that with sufficient practice, even the most ignorant recruit could eventually master them. Days would be spent in learning how to disassemble, clean, oil, and then reassemble a rifle. With luck, the recruits would also remember the names of the rifle parts and how each functioned.

The same instructional model, with little changed other than the participants and the content, dominates reading instruction today in America's schools. Learning to read has been reduced to a process of mastering a series of narrow, specific, hierarchical skills. Where armed-force recruits learn the components of a rifle or the intricacies of close-order drill "by the numbers," recruits to reading learn its mechanics sound by sound and word by word.

For the adults involved, the new system solved the problem of proving to the government that it was getting its money's worth. They could show, by test results, that what children could not do when school started in September they could do the following June. For example, they could recognize a "short *a*" when they saw it in a three-letter word. Learning had indeed taken place.

The problem is that children can acquire thousands of such skills, and yet these skills won't add up to reading. It's as though a mortician was brought in to perform an autopsy on reading. By the time he has finished cutting up the body, no one can recognize it, let alone discern how it once fit together into a working whole.

It's true, the programs *can* teach the "system." But they cannot reach beneath the surface of any child to generate the kind of personal dedication that ultimately makes a reader, or instill the sense of discovery, unlock mysteries, create the feeling of empathy, and all of the other things reading does to produce pleasure.

There is little, if any, pleasure in the performance of these by-the-numbers tasks.

Only the weakest connection is made between such automated learning and reading itself.

Children do not come to think of reading as intrinsically valuable. Instead, they associate it almost exclusively with the educational equivalent of manual labor.

In America's schools today, three decades after Sputnik, reading instruction is as impersonal and lacking in the excitement of discovery and accomplishment as was the acquisition of skills by those World War II recruits. The children move through sequenced reading stages as they might learn close-order drill, their progress carefully noted on "continuums" that list hundreds of minute skills they must acquire—skills that, even when assembled, rarely produce lifelong readers.

No one disputes that somewhere along the way a child has to learn what letters stand for and how series of letters combine into words. The preschool years are an ideal time for such instruction, because three- and four-year-olds enjoy the repetition of simple tasks. First-graders may even sit still for such basic work, so excited are they about being in school. But by the second or third grade at the latest, most children will have learned all they'll ever need to know about what letters stand for and how letters become words, and they will become disenchanted with this system. By the fourth grade most of them—your child included—will encounter reading's "wall of pain."

The wall of pain: Anyone familiar with marathon running will recognize this expression. It's a description of what happens to runners about three-quarters through the race. They are suddenly seized with a fatigue so overpowering that they are often unable to go on. As readers, young children reach that point considerably sooner. In the second and third grades, they may simply be bored. By the fourth grade indifference has grown into aversion to reading in any form.

In under four years a child is transformed from an eager learner to a problem student. *Is this a normal development?*

The commonly held view among psychologists is that learning is an automatic and continuous process stemming from the desire of human beings to understand the world in which they live. If this theory is correct, and I believe it is, the deadening of curiosity and a compulsion to learn is completely counter to human nature. Yet exactly such a "death" occurs within millions of American schoolchildren.

Most of the students I interviewed in the course of my research recalled that in the first grade they had positive feelings about reading and about themselves as learners but that they developed increasingly negative feelings as they moved through the grades. Many of those negative feelings remain, even among those who have overcome whatever deficiencies they once had.

"Studies have consistently demonstrated that as elementary-grade students progress in grade level they tend to become less and less interested in school," Michael J. Breen, school psychologist of the West Bend, Wisconsin, Joint School District, noted a few years ago in the professional journal *Education.* "Children tend to start with favorable attitudes toward almost everything related to school but somehow become progressively unenthusiastic." A study conducted by the Bureau of Educational Research at Winona State University, Winona, Minnesota, concluded that the decrease of interest in school on the part of children correlated with their progression through the grades: the higher the grade, the lower their interest.

But something else, in addition to boredom, is encountered at reading's wall of pain. *That something is fear.*

During the 1970s three Ohio educators, Dorothea H. Brown of the Columbus Public Schools, Ann W. Engin of Ohio State University, and Fred H. Wallbrown of Kent State University, made a study of the reading attitudes of intermediate-grade students in the Columbus public schools. They found that the tendency for students to become emotionally upset and experience unpleasant physical sensations or feelings when thinking about or engaging in reading-type activities increased from grade four to grade five. "Somewhere between grades five and six," they reported, "anxiety seems to drop off and remain at a level which is still significantly above where it was originally at grade four."

Anxiety? Emotional upset? Unpleasant physical sensations? What place have such conditions in a learning environment? What are these "reading-type activities" that generate such negative feelings, and what impact will these feelings have on the learning prospects for your child?

Negative emotions have absolutely no place in a learning environment. To the extent that they exist, they can hinder and even cripple your child's capacity to learn. As to what is producing them, my research and observations, coupled with those of numbers of colleagues, leave me without any doubt. In a word, the answer is *testing*.

Until Sputnik, classroom tests had been used primarily by teachers to achieve specific purposes relating to their instruction and their students' absorption of it. How well had the students learned what they had been taught? What hadn't they learned? Once teachers knew those answers, they could design review lessons that would help fill in the gaps.

When I began teaching in 1950, there was a strong, direct link between testing and classroom objectives—objectives based on teachers' on-the-spot assessments of their pupils' educational needs. Four years later I resigned my position to accompany my husband on a journalistic odyssey through the United States, Latin America, and Europe. Except for two years when I taught in France, where a child's destiny is decided by a few points on a national examination, I had no further experience with testing until I returned to the United States in 1970. I quickly discovered that during the years I had been absent from American schools, the process of sorting and judging children had been legitimized and incorporated into the educational structure, almost entirely in response to government requirements.

The intrusion of the government had been gradual. No sudden takeover had coincided with the government's post-Sputnik passion for better education. But as the initial testing programs undertaken in the late fifties and early sixties revealed greater and greater discrepancies between children's desired and actual levels of reading skills, both national and state governments began to offer funds to local school districts for new programs, new materials, and new personnel. With the funds, of course, came new demands for accountability—which meant more and more tests.

The need to come out well enough to retain governmental aid money, but not so well as to lose the special funds, began to consume administrators and dictate their most pressing educational goals. By the seventies, the nation's schools, whether they liked it or not, were caught up in a national achievement test competition, and the educational decisions they made began to seem more and more like expediencies or compromises made to guarantee funding than to advance learning.

Because so much of the testing process is centered on reading, reading itself gains a negative connotation in the minds of children.

The negative impact of testing is all pervasive. In classrooms, students have been so turned off by the endless series of tests that many school districts have had to resort to carnival-like tricks to get them to school on testing days. In September 1980 one district induced its pupils to undergo five days of testing by promising that all students who came to school all five days would be eligible for a raffle. The prize: ice cream. Many teachers report exactly what I myself have observed: the tension and anxiety that accompany twice-yearly achievement tests is so great that pupils' good feelings about their school abilities, painstakingly built up over many months, can be undone in a single morning. On testing day I would bring huge boxes of pretzels into my classroom and allow the children to dip into them at will. It helped, but not much. There were still trembling muscles, fights, angry words, sullen hostility.

In schools today tests are given with such frequency it often seems that they, and not learning, are the purpose for which children are present. Children in regular primary classrooms can anticipate a quiz after each small segment of instruction. Since proceeding to the next segment is dependent on passing the quiz, the pressure is intense. If they fail, they become "special"—with all the psychological consequences such categorization produces. In educational parlance, they are immediately categorized as remedial. In schools with reading specialists, they may be sent for special help to pass the quiz they have failed. But that simple little operation becomes a catch-22. If the children who are sent for special help fall too far behind as a result of missing their regular classroom instruction, they may soon find themselves permanently classified as remedial students. Often the consequence of this reclassification is a self-fulfilling one: the children so reassigned then perform poorly on the annual standardized tests—at which point they become candidates for batteries of psychological tests whose results will determine whether they are to be assigned to special classes that are still further from the educational mainstream.

Even if they stay in the mainstream, today's students must continually confront the prospect of failure. Aside from their daily practice quizzes and the tests that measure mastery of a given set of reading skills, there is an ever-increasing quantity of state and local reading achievement tests, as well as diagnostic, aptitude, and proficiency tests administered when they move to each higher grade.

In our achievement-oriented society, even those children who are above the norm but below the upper 20 percent of students are often treated as though they, too, have learning problems.

Is it any wonder that even the brightest children find the pressures excruciating? Is it any wonder that, though they may learn to read, they seldom become lifelong readers? Who among us will repeatedly and willingly make efforts in which they have little or no confidence and from which they gain little or no enjoyment? No one—children least of all!

No child, no matter how successful, can run the emotional gauntlet of today's primary and secondary schools without being affected. There is scarcely a child in school today who would not be a better reader and a more interested student if he or she were being educated in a calm and positive environment.

Whatever intellectual expectations even the brightest children might have had when they initially set out for school have been quickly dashed and all but destroyed. Thanks to our educational technology, they have been convinced that reading is difficult and dull and that it bears almost no relationship to what they need or want to know. The bridge that might have spanned the distance between what they know from direct experience and what they could know from the vicarious experience offered by reading has never been constructed.

So I conclude that whatever ailed the schools when Sputnik sent off alarms in American education, it was not as bad as the cure.

As parents, we can press our educators and policymakers to recognize that the mass production of reading failures in our schools today is due not to faulty children but to a faulty system of reading instruction. But we can't afford to wait for the system to be changed. If our children are to become lifelong readers, or even adequate readers, we must act now, while they are in the learning stage.

That's why I've written this book. My promise to you is that when you have finished reading it, you will know how to help your child become a reader for life.

CHAPTER ONE

You Can Teach Your Child to Read

Dreams, books, are each a world; and books, we know,
Are a substantial world, both pure and good.
Round these, with tendrils strong as flesh and blood,
Our pastime and our happiness will grow.
—William Wordsworth, *Personal Talk*

FOR AS LONG AS THERE HAVE BEEN SCHOOLS, educators have shrouded the process of learning to read in a dense mystique.

Whether they say so in so many words or whether they imply it, the attitude they broadcast to parents is, "Don't teach your child to read. Let us professionals do it, because you parents will muck it up."

I once held this attitude myself. As a teacher I counseled parents to keep their hands off and leave the teaching to me. As a parent, I followed the dictum, too. I loved literature and shared that love with my two children in our daily story sessions. But I failed to share my knowledge of how to read. I had been taught during teacher training that children arrived at some magical time when they were ready to read. Any attempt to teach them to read before that time was supposedly fraught with psychological and even physiological danger—for example, preschool reading could seriously injure a child's vision! There was no real evidence to indicate that preschool instruction by parents was harmful, but educators had concluded from a single study headed by a prestigious leader of the Progressive Education movement that children younger than six and a half weren't intellectually, linguistically, or physically competent to read.

Over the years I have come to believe that the idea that parents can't teach is propaganda put out by the educational establishment in an unconscious effort to defend its territory. You don't need any special skills or magical materials or electronic devices to make a child a reader. Those have all been developed as *management* tools—tools whose primary purpose is to keep large groups of children from bouncing off the ceiling while they wait for their teachers' attention. Dozens of studies in the last twenty-five years have shown that parents do teach their children how to read before age six. And they do it without benefit of teaching licenses or reading systems.

Steinberg Report on Early Reading

At six months of age, the boy was presented with written material. At three and one-half he was reading short sentences. At four years eleven months he performed satisfactorily on reading tests normally given to children several years his senior. At eight years, his reading level equalled or surpassed that of students four years older in vocabulary and comprehension and his reading rate and precision equalled that of students twice his age.
—Danny Steinberg and Miho Steinberg, Visible Language.

The only skill you needed when you helped your child learn to talk was to know how to talk yourself. When you leaned toward your child with a spoonful of baby food and said "chicken" or "carrots" or "Open, sesame," you were teaching her oral language. Your teaching was as natural as your child's learning. It required no tools or gimmicks or professionally prepared lessons. Reading is no different. The only skill you need when you help your child to become a reader is to know how to read yourself. You certainly don't need a teaching credential or other degree.

The fact is that you are far more qualified than any teacher to deliver the most significant message about reading that your child will ever receive. The message is that language, whether oral or written, contributes to the excitement, fullness, and joy of life. You communicate that message in the simplest possible manner: by sharing language with your child in a positive way.

Children direct a good part of their early lives toward their parents. They are fascinated by the adult world. They ask questions and want to be included. Their absorption, curiosity, and enthusiasm make them ideal pupils. Nor do they come to the relationship empty-handed. They have their own worlds of peers, activities, thoughts, and feelings to describe, and what they communicate, when encouraged to do so, not only strengthens the bonds between them and their parents but convinces them that communication is the key to relationships.

The Special Language of Literature

When parents read to their children or tell them stories, the children are exposed to words and language patterns, such as repetitions and rhyme, that are simply nonexistent in the speech we use to express ourselves most of the time. When a parent sings a lullaby over a baby's crib, that is different from ordinary parent-child communication. Such formalized language patterns are the basis of all literature, and experiences with them are the forerunners of a child's reading development.

The simple nursery rhymes and lullabies that have been the staples of parent-child interactions for centuries are the perfect medium through which small children can start to learn about the written language. Imagine this commonplace scene: A parent is holding an infant on his or her lap and chanting "Pat-a-cake, pat-a-cake, baker's man. Bake me a cake as fast as you can. Pat it and roll it and mark it with a 'B' . . ." The parent guides the baby's hands in patting, rolling, and marking as the baby looks on attentively. ". . . and throw it in the oven for baby and me." The parent flings open the child's arms at the moment of the dramatic climax. For children this ritual is a never-ending delight. It does much more than simply entertain. It helps them to learn about the language forms they will encounter in books. It is all there in this simple nursery rhyme: the formal structure, the patterns of sound and rhythm, the logical development of ideas, the drama. They quickly learn that there is a connection between the sounds they hear and the movement we help them to execute. They learn to anticipate the moment of climax and to respond without our help, because they make the link between the message and themselves. At the same time they develop a sense of literary form that is crucial both to the understanding and the appreciation of the written word in all its forms and with all its purposes.

> *Children must have two fundamental insights before they can learn to read. These two insights are rarely discussed in the research literature on reading and are generally ignored in reading instruction, which may even suppress the insights in children who have already managed to acquire them. Without these insights, reading instruction will remain incomprehensible to children and have the adverse effect of making nonsense of reading.*
>
> *The two fundamental insights are (1) that print is meaningful and (2) that written language is different from speech.*
> —*Frank Smith*, Essays into Literacy

What is so miraculous about all this learning is that it isn't formally taught. It simply happens. It requires no special talent on the part of the parent "teacher." All that is needed is interest.

The reading relationship is a natural outgrowth of a positive personal relationship between parent and child. When a parent reads to an infant child, she transmits both love and knowledge. The initial knowledge, on which all else is built, is that print has significance.

In a study comparing kindergarten children's knowledge, those who knew a lot about written language had parents who believed that it was their responsibility to seize opportunities to convey information about written language to their children. Parents of children who had little knowledge did not share this belief.
—Becoming a Nation of Readers, *report of the Commission on Reading, National Institute of Education*

A book that involves children actively with written messages is a wonderful way to develop the insight that print has significance. When our first child, Linden, was only a few months old, I chanced upon a book called *Pat the Bunny* by Dorothy Kunhardt. As I held Linden on my lap, I guided her hand in accordance with the instructions on each page. "Pat the bunny," page one directed. Pat, pat, pat went Linden's hand. Another page contained a drawing of a man's face with sandpaper pasted to it. "Feel Daddy's beard," the caption instructed, and I moved Linden's tiny forefinger back and forth across the scratchy surface. On other pages, Linden would be told to stroke the bunny's furry hide or look at the baby in the tiny mirror. Before long Linden's hand didn't have to be guided. She herself would respond to the words I read to her; whether she actually understood the words is immaterial; she knew that some magical association existed between the words, the pictures, and her response. Our family went through three copies of *Pat the Bunny* before the book had lost its fascination, but by that time, the habit of responding to print was well established in Linden's mind.

Later our children would add a set of literary references

to their sensitivity to literary form—references that would aid them in their own reading as well as in life. They would come gradually to know which kinds of acts described in the books were sure to be praised and which punished, how the good and bad characters will act, what people do in specific circumstances, how they relate to one another.

In the end, it is not reading systems that make children readers. Children become readers when they receive the kind of emotional and intellectual nourishment around reading that only a caring adult can give.

Most of us carry with us memories of being read to as children. Your parents may not have read books to you, but chances are that they sat on the floor with you on Sunday morning and read you the funny papers. Or perhaps they read you the print on the cereal box, the directions that came with a new toy, or the instructions on a sign. Whatever form it took, the reading of parent to child was, for all of us, one of the treasured rites of childhood. If it meant that much to us as children, it will mean no less to our own children. And it will give us, as parents, a new set of memories to treasure and carry with us, in addition to the satisfaction of having initiated in our children the desire to learn to read.

Parents play roles of inestimable importance in laying the foundation for learning to read. A parent is a child's first tutor in unraveling the fascinating puzzle of written language. A parent is a child's one source of faith that somehow, sooner or later, he or she will become a good reader.
—Becoming a Nation of Readers, *report of the Commission on Reading, National Institute of Education*

As you will see in chapter 2, there are many different ways to introduce children to the world of reading. Whatever the form it takes, the reading by you to your child will be a special, private event, an event that can join you and your child in a way that will nourish you both.

Why You're So Well Qualified to Make Your Child a Reader

Whatever else they may be, parents are their children's first and most important teachers. They teach them how to talk and provide them with the very foundation of language, the two most vital resources the children will ever acquire. At that point, almost all parents stop, because they have been led to believe that they are unqualified to teach. In most cases, this makes no sense at all.

Let me list just a few of the advantages you as a parent have in teaching your child to read:

1. You have access to your child in her most fruitful language-learning years. You are there at the very moment when your child discovers the incredible power of words to communicate what she wants, how she is feeling, and what she has learned. Because you are there at that moment, you can capitalize on your child's enthusiasm and capabilities.

2. You can give learning a positive emotional dimension by injecting your love and care into the reading situation. As warm and dedicated as some teachers may be, none of them is going to feel what you feel for your own child or be able to invest that feeling into the teaching process. To the contrary, your child is apt to find her teacher to be remote in comparison to the genuine attention she is used to getting from you. The mere fact of your being at home is another strong plus in your favor. For a child, a classroom can be an uncomfortable environment, even though it may be loaded with friends.

3. You can personalize your child's reading program by building on her interests. Many teachers ask children what they're interested in, and then either don't listen to the answers or forget them within the hour. They are simply too busy, and too fragmented by the needs

of thirty different children, to be able to learn about and take advantage of the interests of a single individual. You, on the other hand, can know absolutely everything about your child's enthusiasms and can bring to bear your concentrated focus to help stimulate them.

4. You can provide an environment that is unstressed. Unlike the schools, whose interactions with children so often cause children to feel as if they are on trial, you can help your child learn to read without her having to worry about the consequences of making mistakes or doing poorly on a reading test. You will be so familiar with your child's reading development that you will know in advance when and where your child will need help. You can provide the cues that will keep her from ever feeling like a reading failure.

Where the schools are trapped in thirty years of institutionalized problems, you are beholden to no administrator or public official and to no instructional system. You are not obligated, as teachers are, to follow strict schedules, teach prescribed skills, and read from required texts. You are free to make any moment of the day a joyous reading experience for your child. You are free, if you wish, to make an immediate positive impact on your child's future as a reader.

I believe that parents with even the slimmest of reading skills who want their children to learn to read can help them get a start *and* encourage them along the way. As to the teaching skills required, my mother told me of how her mother, who had completed only the primary grades, taught her father, who'd had no schooling at all, to read. She did this by identifying letters and words for him in their mail-order catalog. She encouraged him to copy words and read them back. When he stumbled, she told him the words again. She did this until he had acquired enough of a reading foundation to be able to proceed on his own.

Sarah's Story

Sarah is the child of two Bear Valley, California, residents, neither of whom had the opportunity to obtain a college degree.

From the day Sarah was born, her mother, Donna, started talking and singing to her. It didn't matter that she got no reaction at first. When Sarah did begin to look at Donna when she heard the sound of her voice, it made it that much more exciting. Donna and her husband, Joel, talked to Sarah about all kinds of things. They'd take her to the window and show her the birds flying outside; they did more than point and say the word *birds*. They talked about what birds were, what they did, where they lived—about almost anything that they could think of. Sarah got the message. Eight months later, the first word to follow the traditional *Mom* and *Dad* was the word *bird*, accompanied by a gesture toward the outside. Donna encouraged the development of Sarah's language. "This is a spoon," she would say, as she handed Sarah the spoon. Having Sarah touch the object as she repeated a new word helped her to understand, Donna believed. Together, they identified everything in sight.

The intensive introduction to the world of words that started early in Sarah's life was not limited just to oral language but included written language as well. At ten months Donna started to read to Sarah. She had waited only long enough for her daughter to be able to sit up on her own. Sarah's exposure to books was continuous. She was read to several times a day. She loved listening to the words and having her parents' undivided attention. It became obvious to the many friends who came to visit Joel and Donna that the one way to captivate Sarah and maintain her attention was to bring out a book and offer to read to her. It worked every time.

At eighteen months, Sarah began to take a favorite book to bed with her. A friend who baby-sat for Donna had been the first to put Sarah into her crib with a book. She hoped to give Sarah something to do before she fell asleep, thereby avoiding the sobs and screams of a child left alone with nothing to do. It worked. It also had an unexpected side effect. It strengthened an already strong attachment to books. Sarah began to insist on having a book before going to bed. In the morning Donna would find Sarah "reading" her books to her dolls. She found that not only was Sarah perfectly happy to remain alone in her crib for up to an hour every morning, the time alone with her books dissipated the usual cranky, just-awakened mood. Donna's show of pleasure when she found Sarah reading reinforced the habit.

At one year and ten months, Sarah began to memorize the books she read most frequently. Looking at the picture she would remember the accompanying sentence and pretend to read. Unaware of this a friend of Joel's sat down to read to Sarah. He opened the book he had chosen to the title page.

"Spring is a new beginning," Sarah announced.

"What did you say?" he asked in disbelief.

"Spring is a new beginning," Sarah repeated. "That's the name of the book."

"Well, if you're so smart," he said, "you read it." She did —from memory, from beginning to end.

By the age of three Sarah was well on her way to being "a reader." Her development came through her own language explorations and discoveries, but she didn't do it alone. Her parents laid the groundwork. Yet no formal training or planning was required; it was all spontaneous and natural. What happened can be expressed in a single word: *interaction.*

Before she reached school, Sarah had already learned the four essentials for independent reading:

First, she had learned to associate oral sounds and concepts with their written equivalents.

Second, she had learned that the written language said something to her.

Third, she had learned that she could anticipate what the words would say before she heard or saw them.

Fourth, she had learned to value reading and writing as sources of entertainment and communication.

Sarah's story is not unusual. She is not a "gifted" child; her parents are not extraordinary teachers. She is an "average" child whose parents paid above-average attention to introducing their child to reading. What those parents did, you can do. What Sarah accomplished, your child can, too.

Perhaps the most important predictor for Sarah's eventual success as a reader is her feeling of excitement about reading. For her, reading has come to be associated with good family times.

Such positive associations are absolutely critical to your child's future as a reader.

The Make-Your-Child-a-Lifelong-Reader Program

This is not a book about teaching your child to read. This is a book on helping your child learn about reading. As you follow the suggestions in the Make-your-child-a-lifelong-reader program, you will be giving your child a sense of what it is to read. You will be helping her learn how to read, not on a mechanical basis but on an intellectual and affective basis—to read with the head and with the heart. And you will be teaching your child to value the process of reading and to want to develop specific processing skills, skills that she will learn either with or without the school's help.

The reading program is divided into three age classifications. The first four chapters all concern the child from infancy to age six. Chapter 2 deals with developing your child's recognition that written words have significance. Chapter 3 deals with developing physical and emotional response to the formal language patterns that children will encounter in reading. Chapter 4 discusses the development of children's intellectual responses to printed language.

Chapter 5 indicates how to nurture the belief that reading is an important part of life.

The chapters all cover the same age range, but they cover it from different perspectives. Each chapter starts at the youngest skills and builds to the oldest, from infancy to age six.

The second phase of the program deals with the reading development of the child from age six to twelve. Chapters 6 and 7 focus on developing a young reader's ability to interact with a text competently and confidently. The final phase relates to the twelve- to seventeen-year-old. Chapter 8 focuses on keeping the reading habit alive during this tumultuous period. Chapter 9 tells parents how to help children make the transition to adult reading.

In each of the chapters you will be given a set of reading goals to meet in developing one basic aspect of the reading process. For each reading goal you will be offered a number of suggestions—simple and natural activities—that you will use in guiding your child's development as a lifelong reader. Not every possible thing will be suggested. You will have your own ideas. I will simply give some basic ideas, so you can carry on from there.

This program was not designed to be followed step by step. You will not do one thing, finish it, then move on to the next thing. Reading development does not occur in discrete and sequential steps any more than spoken language development does. We know in general that children learn to read simple words before they learn to read sentences, but that doesn't mean that we don't build up sentence knowledge until all the words have been learned. To stimulate your child's reading development, you need to give her as extensive an array of language opportunities as you possibly can. Your child will take advantage of whatever of those opportunities she can.

You need not worry about giving your child something that is not appropriate for her level of development. There is nothing in this program that is going to pressure your child.

If you give her something she is too young for, she will simply ignore it. If she's not interested in looking at the horse on page two, she simply won't look at it, and you will give up. You will be able to recognize your own child's stage of development as you try out the suggestions.

You will be given a number of language goals to meet in each of the three phases of the program. Since many of the goals will be developed simultaneously, it is important for you to read all of the chapters that relate to the age level of your child.

Ideally you would start this reading program in the first weeks of your child's life. But if that's not possible (because at this reading your child is already two or eight or fourteen), she can still benefit from the program. If your child is entering the program at age ten, let's say, you will want to read the goals and suggestions presented for the youngest group, as well as those for the middle group. If you discover that your child has not yet achieved some of the goals of phase one of the program, you will want to work with her on these. Just adapt the materials you use to her level of maturity. And at the same time, continue to work on some of the goals at her appropriate age level. If your child is advanced in her reading development, you will want to test the next higher age bracket for your goals and activities.

In addition to the techniques I'm going to give you for helping your child develop reading prowess, I'm going to show you how to help your child. I say *help* and not *correct* because I'm not interested in your correcting your child. I know you are going to do it, but when you do, I want you to do it in ways that are least apt to create tension, unhappiness, and fear of making mistakes—none of which are helpful to your child's growth and progress.

As you proceed you might want to keep in mind some of the justified concerns the schools have had over the years about parents teaching their children to read.

The schools' greatest concern is for the child's psychological well-being. They believe that many parents do not interact with their children in a constructive fashion in instructional situations. Some parents have a tendency to overwhelm their youngsters with help, thereby making them overly dependent. Other parents don't help enough, thereby frustrating the child. The result of both of these extremes of helping behavior is that the child develops a distaste for learning to read.

Schools fear the unreal expectations that many parents hold for their children's achievement. They feel that parents often make assessments of children's ability or maturity that are either exaggerated or depreciated and that these assessments set young readers up for failure—failure that often results in children's negative attitudes about reading itself and about themselves as readers.

Along the same lines, schools fear the pressure that parents sometimes exert in their zeal for their children to excel, pressure that often comes in the form of unfavorable comparisons with siblings and playmates. They feel that such pressure creates an aversion to reading.

These are legitimate concerns. Without the proper guidance, children's progress in learning to read can be impeded. These are things that you, in helping your child become a reader, need to be careful about. By being aware of the pitfalls, you can avoid the mistakes that some parents make.

In teaching, as in loving, the course doesn't always run smooth. There will be times when you will doubt your ability to transfer your knowledge to your child. But don't blame your inexperience or lack of formal training as a teacher; even the best-trained and most gifted teachers experience such moments of doubts. In such times it will help you to remember that your child is the most forgiving person you know. He or she wants your help, as well as the love it represents.

PART ONE

FROM INFANCY to AGE SIX:
Building a Reading Base

CHAPTER TWO

Showing Your Child That Written Words Have Significance

Child of the pure unclouded brow
And dreaming eyes of wonder!
Though time be fleet, and I and thou
Are half a life asunder,
Thy loving smile will surely hail
The love-gift of a fairy-tale.
—Lewis Carroll, *Through the Looking-Glass*

MAKING YOUR CHILD A READER may sound like an overwhelming task. But, as you will see, the steps toward that goal are simply an extension of the very same language instruction you have conducted naturally and effortlessly from the earliest days of your child's life.

The techniques you used to teach your baby to call you Mama and Daddy and himself Baby are the very techniques you will use when you teach him to read those words.

Let's review how you probably taught your baby the spoken word for the animals that we call dogs. It will help you to recognize what you know intuitively about teaching your spoken language to your children. It will help you to apply the same techniques to helping your children learn to read.

When you wanted your child to learn the word *dog,* you did three things: You showed him what a dog was; you said the sound that corresponds to that concept; and you taught him how to make the sounds themselves.

Chances are this is the way you did it:

When you saw a dog, whether running across the street or appearing on TV or in magazines and books, you drew your baby's attention to it. At the same time, you said, "dog." And you prompted your baby to repeat the sound you had made. You must have done this a hundred times, perhaps more. Who knows? You didn't count. You didn't think of what you were doing as teaching. You just shared something you knew.

Your sharing was unsullied by performance expectations. If, in the course of language-learning sessions, your baby called a horse a dog, you probably laughed and repeated the joke to your parents and friends. You weren't cross or upset with your baby. You were thrilled that your child had grasped at least part of the concept of "dog." You continued to identify dogs—dogs of all colors, all sizes and shapes—and to prompt your child to do the same, until your child could correctly identify and say, "dog."

If you step back and analyze your teaching—which is what it really was—you'll discover that it incorporated five of the ingredients that learning specialists agree are so important for learning. You identified your goal. You provided plenty of time for the learning. You demonstrated correct responses. You supported all your baby's efforts. And most important, your teaching was caring and accepting.

As a result of both the experiences you provided and the manner in which you presented them, your child quickly learned to call an animal with a certain set of characteristics a dog. Yet the procedures you used to teach him that complicated intellectual feat were so simple that you probably never gave them a second thought.

The process is no more complicated or scholastic when you teach children the written word that stands for the concept of dog.

How do you do it? You use exactly the same procedures you used when you taught your child to speak: You direct his attention to a written word. You say the word. You encourage him to say the word. The only difference is that now you are focusing on written words instead of on spoken ones.

Procedures for Helping Your Child Make Associations Between Spoken and Written Words

- *Direct his attention to a written word.*
- *Say the word.*
- *Encourage him to repeat the word.*
- *Repeat the process whenever the opportunity naturally presents itself.*

In the following sections I will outline your reading goals and give you specific suggestions for things you can do to move your children along toward these goals. I will also explain why I am asking you to do these things. I will endeavor to provide you with enough information so that you will be able to build upon my basic ideas to create a personalized reading program for your child. I will also tell you what materials you need to work with and suggest ways of working with children that have been found effective for parents and teachers.

Goal 1: Developing an Awareness of Written Words

For very young children a written word has no inherent attraction. If they notice it at all—and chances are they will not—it will most likely seem a part of a relatively uninteresting design. Only when you make them aware that a word design refers to something both you and they care about will they pay any attention to it.

> *While it is traditional for oral language to be acquired first and for the acquisition of reading to build on oral language, it does not have to be this way. In fact, when two modes of language are learned concurrently, each mode builds on the other and enriches the other. The total language base is expanded.*
> —*Thelma E. Weeks, Institute for Language Development, Palo Alto, California*

Even before your baby's babbling changes from a mere repetition of sounds ("da-da-da-da-da") to words that represent a clear idea ("Dada") you need to begin to draw his attention to written words.

SUGGESTION: Point out and read to your child the words that are important to him.

The most basic thing you can do to develop awareness of written words is to call your child's attention to those words that have special meaning, words that carry an emotional charge. The big word on the Cheerios box was such a word for little Sarah, the eighteen-month-old in Bear Valley, California, because she adored Cheerios. When the words *Sesame Street* flash on the television screen, they evoke a delighted response from the program's small fans. Your child will have his own special, emotion-laden words upon which you can draw to help him notice written words and begin to make correct associations between the words he hears and the words he sees.

Important, pleasurable words will usually name a thing or person that your child especially cares about. *Baby* and *Mommy* and *Daddy* are all very important words for a young child. So are the names of favorite foods, toys, and other possessions. In this age of graphics, you won't have to search far to find a boldly printed supply of words important enough to capture and maintain your child's interest. They will be on the food containers on your kitchen shelves, on the toys in the nursery, on the clothes your child wears, and in the TV programs he watches. Even if your home lacks books, it still abounds with words that will evoke your child's responses.

Surround the children with written symbols as of the first years of their lives, symbols that are significantly related to objects: they will learn to read just as they learned to speak.
—*L. Stevens and R. C. Orem,* The Case for Early Reading

All you need to do with these ready-made words is draw your child's attention to them as you say them aloud —exactly as you did when you wanted your child to learn a spoken word. Then prompt your child to say the word.

At first your child will just be mimicking your vocal sounds and will pay little attention to the written word. But as you repeat the process, he will gradually discover the link between what you are saying and the word he is seeing.

In these early stages, be sure to show your young child you are pleased with any attention he gives to words. A pat or a smile will suffice.

SUGGESTION: Label your child's special belongings and the places where they are kept.

Labeling is a procedure that has been going on for a long time in the schools. It was particularly popularized in Glenn Doman's book *How to Teach Your Baby to Read.* (New York: Random House, 1964.)

You can vastly expand your child's opportunity to become aware of words if you use your Magic Marker liberally to label his special belongings.

Words become exciting to a young child when they

indicate that something is his very own. Words that identify a toy box as "SUSIE'S TOY BOX" and a towel as "SEAN'S HAND TOWEL" are special, important words to Susie and Sean. Such labels seem to be endowed with even greater emotional value than the words that label things that give pleasure—perhaps because of a certain status they confer upon the youngster.

There are four points to bear in mind as you make your labels:

1. Print the letters.

2. Use capital letters for only the beginning letter of a proper noun, such as Jane or Harry.

3. Make your letters large, so your child can see them from a distance. A small letter like *o* or *m* should be at least ¾ inch tall. A tall letter like *b* or a capital letter like *A* should be 1½ inches tall.

4. Put no more than three words on a label.

Just adding more words to an environment that is already rich in words is not enough. You need to show off the words to your Susie or your Sean. And you need to talk about them.

Asking questions and giving directions are natural ways to direct children's attention to labeled objects. "Where is your towel, Sean?" or "Put your blocks in the toy box, Susie," are examples of the kinds of word guidance that will help Susie and Sean quickly to become aware of the relationships between idea, sound, and written word.

The labeling process becomes even more attractive to your child when you let him "label" some household object. Very young children will be incapable of doing the actual labeling, but if you ask them what they want to label and then write the label for them to stick up, they will feel like they have done it themselves. For a three- or four-year-old child who has reached the copying stage, write the words that the child requests and let him copy them onto a long strip of paper. A roll of adding machine tape is perfect for this. It makes it possible for your child to write labels of varying sizes and not feel constrained by the length of the paper with which he has to work.

SUGGESTION: Point out and read words to your child when you are outside your home.

When your child is in his second year you can begin to broaden his awareness of written words by focusing his attention on words you encounter when you are out and about. Even a routine trip to the supermarket or the laundromat can become a word-awareness adventure for your child if, along the way, you point out the traffic signs, the advertisements, and the names of buildings.

Early development of the knowledge required for reading comes from experience talking and learning about the world and talking and learning about written language.
—Becoming a Nation of Readers, *report of the Commission on Reading, National Institute of Education*

The most natural way to focus your child's attention on public words is to talk about them. As you approach the school zone, tell your child that the school crossing guard's sign says "Stop." And tell him why the guard is there and what you, the driver, must do as a consequence. Or explain that you have to go to the bank for some money and then point out the name of the bank to your youngster as you approach the building. In short, get him involved in the activity. Awaken him to the words that are related to it. It is easier to stick with nouns because these are what a young child uses most often in speech.

When you reach your destination, you want to continue to involve your child with words. As you are shopping tell your child what you are looking for and, even if he is too young to be of any help, pretend to engage him in the search for favorite foods. When your child is older, let him really help you find the things you want and take them from the shelf. In each case, make sure you point out and say the name of the item as you find it. And don't forget to show your pleasure in your youngster's collaboration.

SUGGESTION: **Read to your child and note the words or phrases to which he responds. Point these out in books.**

Since your ultimate goal is to make your child a reader of books and other connected material, it is important for you early on in your word-awareness program to introduce your child to books.

The books that are written for the very young are perfect for developing word awareness. Often just the sound of their simple rhymes, stories, and messages is enough to mesmerize babies. If you add to that the warm presence of a loving parent, you have a word environment to which young children really respond.

You can take best advantage of this situation by noting those words or phrases that cause your child to perk up, or laugh, or show other signs of interest. If you are reading "Bow, wow, wow. Whose dog art thou? Little Tom Tinker's dog. Bow, wow, wow," chances are your child will respond by making the dog sounds that you taught him to make when you first taught the word *dog.* Or he may mimic your "Bow, wow, wow" or pat the book as though it were the dog it brings to mind. These words then become your working words.

Every time you come to one of these words or phrases in the book you are reading, make them stand out. Use your voice to accentuate them. Before long, your child will begin to indicate to you where those key words and phrases are in the story. When that happens, show him that you are impressed with his cleverness.

Don't expect real word recognition in this awareness phase. When two-year-old Carrie, the daughter of friends, brought me her book and sat down to "read" it to me, there was no question at all in her mind that she was reading. Her finger moved under the words on each page as she told her favorite story about a kitten. If the words she said happened to match the words on the page, it was pure coincidence. Obviously Carrie was many experiences away from being able to recognize written words, but she amply demonstrated that she was aware that there were words on the page that corresponded to spoken language.

She had mastered her first reading goal, awareness of written words.

Goal 2: Associating Spoken and Written Words

Associations between oral and written language are an integral part of written-word awareness. As children become aware that the designs they see on boxes and toys and T-shirts have some meaning, they start to verbalize that meaning. They extend their language knowledge beyond the mere linkage of concept and sound, to the more complex linkage of concept, sound, and written symbol. The more they are helped to notice these correspondences, the more adept they become at making the associations themselves.

At first, children need your help to stimulate their desire to make those associations, just as they needed it when they learned to link the concept of dog with the sound symbol that represented it. Directing their attention to a written word as you say it makes them aware of words and their meanings.

SUGGESTION: **Encourage your child to look at and say words that have some special meaning.**

Encouraging children to say a word as they look at it helps build associations between spoken and written words. Repetition is essential for building enduring associations. But rote repetition of the kind provided in most school settings is both boring to children and unproductive. To be productive, repetitions need to be enjoyable and, whenever possible, need to serve some objective other than the teaching objective.

One of the simplest ways for you to stimulate your child to make word and sound associations is to read to him from the labels on foodstuffs that he especially likes or the labels that you have affixed to his personal belongings. The rest of the procedure is identical to the one you used when you taught your child how to speak. Just focus his attention on the word by pointing to it. Then encourage your child to say the word.

Echoing your words will seem like a game to your youngster—a game he will particularly enjoy if you show your enthusiasm over his efforts.

SUGGESTION: **Use starter books to help your child make the connection between spoken and written words.**

A favorite starter book like *Pat the Bunny* by Dorothy Kunhardt, which I described in chapter 1, also makes a perfect tool for encouraging your child to make sound and print associations. Just read the one or two words on each page as you point to them. Then pause and wait for your child to mimic you. If that response is not spontaneous, just pose a simple question like, "What's this?" as you point to the picture on the page. Or "Who's that?"

Almost anything you do to encourage repetition is enjoyable for youngsters when they feel they are partners in an enterprise.

SUGGESTION: **Have your child supply some of the words in the stories or rhymes that you read.**

One of the most engaging of enterprises occurs when your child joins you in "reading" words. Our sixteen-month-old daughter was a study in absorption and glee when she supplied the words we left out as we read her favorite rhymes and stories. Among her favorite words were those that indicated that a character or an object in a story was very small. So these were the words we always left for her to supply when we read. As she followed *The Story of the Three Bears,* by Eleanor Mure, she would listen attentively to each bear's speech, just waiting for us to pause so she could insert the words "Little Wee Bear" and "little wee voice" in the appropriate places. This was a favorite word partnership for both our children from the time they were very tiny until they were well launched as readers.

The words you will want to leave for your child to say can be the working words you found earlier, the words to which he had noticeably responded in earlier readings of stories or rhymes.

> *What the child who is least ready for systematic reading instruction needs most is ample experience with oral and printed language, and early opportunities to begin to write.*
> —Becoming a Nation of Readers, *report of the Commission on Reading, National Institute of Education*

Engaging successfully in making language associations fills children with delight and pride in accomplishment that buoys them through endless repetitions of the same exercise.

Goal 3: Developing Word-Producing Skills

Everything you do to develop word awareness and associations between oral and written language will be enhanced by opportunities you offer your child to actually write words. But before children can experience any degree of success, they need to learn to manipulate the tools that they will use for writing.

Note that I said *they need to learn*—not *you need to teach.* Children develop the coordination that enables them to control a pencil or crayon or paintbrush and paper at their own individual rates; each of them is different. In a roomful of nursery school children, approximately a third will be adept with crayon and paper; a third will be able to just manage to use them, albeit clumsily; and a third will produce only uncontrolled scribbles. To attempt to teach these skills is to interfere with natural maturation processes and to frustrate children unnecessarily.

Writing is important in its own right. Because of the interrelatedness of language, learning to write also aids in reading development. For many young children, the desire to communicate provides an incentive for using written language. In an investigation of children who read before they entered first grade, the parents described these children as "paper-and-pencil kids." For some, in fact, learning to read was a by-product of interest in writing.
—Becoming a Nation of Readers, *report of the Commission on Reading, National Institute of Education*

Tiny children love the movement involved in putting marks on large pieces of paper and the end results, no matter what they are like. At this stage they want neither your help nor your suggestions about color, form, or control.

The best way to help children develop the fine motor and eye-hand coordination skills they will need when they form letters is to give them access to a variety of materials as early as they show an interest. Then let them have at it. They will learn from doing.

SUGGESTION: **Give your child materials for writing.**

Scribbling without form or boundary will be your child's first response to crayons and paper. Let him scribble to his heart's content. It's a good way for him to get acquainted with the materials and to begin to develop the skills he needs for forming letters. Fat crayons and any kind of paper will do to start. Finger painting on flattened-out paper bags is another application of a medium to paper that is easy and pleasing to even the most unskilled tot. It also anticipates the act of writing and helps him to develop control for that more advanced activity.

SUGGESTION: **Provide your child with alphabet blocks.**

In order to produce words, a child must have had some experience with the letters of the alphabet. One of the most time-proven ways to help children learn something about letters is to provide them with simple, old-fashioned alphabet blocks. The virtue of these blocks is that they don't require the kind of coordination that other word-producing activities require. Therefore, they are perfect for a toddler's first efforts to write. A toddler can build simple words like *cat* and *dog* and *baby* with blocks long before he can control a pencil or crayon sufficiently well to print those words. And the satisfaction this gives a tiny tot is enormous.

Observations from a Study of Children Who Learn to Read Early

Almost without exception the starting point of curiosity about written language was an interest in scribbling and drawing. From this developed interest in copying objects and letters of the alphabet. When a child was able to copy letters —and not all the children who had the interest developed the skill—his almost inevitable request was, "Show me my name."

—*Dolores Durkin,* Children Who Read Early

Alphabet blocks serve a variety of functions. First of all, they are perfect props for helping you to develop your child's letter awareness. As you help your child build with blocks or oversee his play, refer to the blocks by their letter names. You might say such things as, "Watch out, the G is falling off." Or "How about putting this S on top?" Any remark that identifies a letter in a playful way helps to build letter awareness.

Later on, alphabet blocks can help you to teach your child to recognize letters and to use them to actually build words. A set of magnetic letters that your child can stick to the stove or refrigerator will keep your child near you when you are working in the kitchen and enable you to assist in the word-building activity. As children's letter awareness develops, their interest in naming letters and in matching them up with words grows. The more you and your child work with the blocks, the sooner he will become a producer of written words.

SUGGESTION: Buy or make an alphabet book.

Another time-tested way to help your child become familiar with letters and their use is to provide him with an alphabet book. If you are buying this book, choose the simplest one you can find. It is far easier for young children to focus on letters and words when they encounter only a few items on a page and when they are not distracted by illustrations. As a general rule, the fewer the items on a page and the fewer and less complex the illustrations, the better your alphabet book will work for developing word-production skills. For a listing of alphabet books refer to the Suggested Reading section at the end of Part One.

You can easily make your own alphabet books with construction paper, pictures of objects cut out of magazines or brochures, and a brightly colored felt marker. As you plan your book, bear these points in mind:

Print only one letter on each 8½-by-11-inch sheet. If you have just one, there is no way your child can become confused. Make your letters at least 2 inches tall.

Print both the capital and small form of each letter. Just as your child learned that a collie and a dachshund were both dogs, he can learn that there are two forms of a single letter and be able to identify them both as A or B. Use the simplest possible lettering style. Think of your letters as combinations of straight sticks and round balls.

Paste on each letter page the picture of one object whose name starts with the letter you have in mind. If possible, you'll want to select objects for which your baby has shown some feeling.

Fasten the pages together so they are easy to turn. Avoid the use of brads and staples, because they can pinch or scratch. Instead, punch holes in the upper left-hand corner of the letter sheet and tie the sheets together with bits of ribbon or yarn.

These homemade books won't last long, but that is all to the good. Replacing old books with new ones that display completely different objects will help keep your child's interest in alphabet discoveries high.

SUGGESTION: Encourage your child to write.

Children need very little fine muscle control or knowledge of the alphabet or of how to spell words to begin to write. All they need is a little encouragement from you.

Your eighteen- to twenty-four-month-old scribbler will relish the opportunity to write, provided he has some guidelines to follow and something on which to write.

Coloring books have a long history as a boon to parents and teachers because they keep young children busy and quiet. They work fine as pacifiers because children like to color. But they also work fine as vehicles for helping children learn to produce words. Therefore, they can be a very useful part of your reading program.

Coloring books usually name in big, bold letters the objects to be colored. Most children, especially those who have become sensitive to words and letters, are eager to copy those letters, thereby providing a label for their drawings. Copying words is an act they will need to perform hundreds of times before they become independent writers.

If your child does not spontaneously copy the words that go along with the designs in the book, all you need do is suggest that you are available to help copy the letters. Or say, "Why don't you write 'house' on your drawing?" And as you point to the word, say, "See, here it is."

If your child's book doesn't have words, you need to print them in big letters so that he will have a model to copy. You can also use magazines, newspapers, and advertising brochures for coloring and copying purposes. Just suggest that your child color or print right over the illustrations and text. Provide brightly colored crayons for the job.

A very young child, given a writing tool and something to write on, will scribble spontaneously and watch his production with great interest. Furthermore, if writing materials are easily available, a child will make use of them on his own. His interest in writing activity may occur in spurts and appear to lag in between, but such spontaneity is probably a good thing. The evidence available indicates that the quality of the scribbling matures by itself. . . . If there are letters and numbers available for copying, children make attempts to copy them and improve with time without correction or adult guidance. The child recognizes the better match himself and gets satisfaction from his improvement.
—Eleanor J. Gibson and Harry Levin, The Psychology of
Reading

I want to caution you again that the same guideline applies in the development of word production as in the development of word awareness: SHARE YOUR KNOWLEDGE, DON'T IMPOSE IT. Give your child the tools, and he will spontaneously build and scribble and color and copy. In the process he will discover for himself how letters and words look and how they fit together to say something. Try to control any urge you might have to turn these exploratory activities into lessons. The moment you begin to force your youngster's learning, you risk ruining his appetite for playing with letters and words.

Chances are you won't be able to read your two-year-old's scrawl. Crucial letters will be left out. Most others will be misshapen. Many will be backwards. But your child will know what he has written. Just ask him to read it to you. Then comment on the contents of the writing rather than the way it was written.

Goal 4: Associating Simple Written Sentences with Spoken Messages

When you taught your child to speak, you emphasized single words like *dog, cat, Mommy,* and *Daddy.* These were words you wanted your child to understand and to speak. But at the same time you were teaching solitary words, you were also teaching language in its connected form. As your spoon approached your child's mouth, you said, "Open up," or "Um, good." At bath time you announced, "It's time for your bath." While you may have concentrated on getting your child to say only single words at first, you still were preparing him to use groups of words to express ideas.

You need to do exactly the same thing when you teach written language. Once children have begun to associate single words with their spoken equivalent, it is time for you to introduce words in the form of simple written sentences.

SUGGESTION: **Write notes to your children.**

Written sentences are not too difficult for a small child, providing they are couched in spoken language patterns with which he is familiar and say something that the child can anticipate. The best of these word patterns is the sentence that expresses your love.

In the early stages, a simple "I love you," written with alphabet blocks or hand printed in large letters in the sandbox or on a finger painting, will not only attract your youngster's attention but delight him as well. When you read a love message to small children, they beam with pleasure. And they quickly learn to associate the string of words with the spoken thought.

Make note writing a habit. Whether your child can read or not, he will understand an "I love you. [signed] Mom (or Dad)" message. Put notes in snacks, on his pillows, in his pockets. You don't need to use outsize paper for these notes, but do print them in large, easy-to-read letters. Make your short letters at least ¼ inch tall. Again, I want to repeat, though tiny children may seem to be able to read these notes, they are not actually reading at first. They cannot be expected to. What they are doing is associating simple written sentences with spoken messages. And perhaps even more important, they are learning that the written message is a source of pleasure.

Every suggestion in this section is geared to elicit exactly this kind of intellectual and emotional response to everyday words and messages. When you drew your child's attention to words on his favorite cereal and wrote labels and love notes, you made everyday written language both relevant and satisfying to your child.

The suggestions in the next section are also designed to ensure your child's response. The only difference is that now you will be focusing on helping your child become personally involved with the more structured language of literature. Your goal: to make sure when your child hears or reads literary language, he will respond.

CHAPTER THREE

Learning to Respond Physically and Emotionally to Literature

> I don't think I was ever disappointed by books. I must have been what any author would consider an ideal reader; I felt every pain and pleasure suffered or enjoyed by all the characters. Oh, but I identified! Or tried to.
>
> —Eudora Welty

WHEN YOUNGSTERS LOOK AT THE WORDS *apple* and *pie* and simply name them, that is word identification. When they preface or follow this act with a "Yum, yum" or a rub of the tummy, they are recalling the delicious taste of apple pie, perhaps even imagining eating a piece of it at that very moment. That is reading.

The process for helping your child experience literary language in this personal way is almost identical to the one you've just learned. First, you ensure that she has contact with the language—in this case, with literature. Sing, recite, or read it to her. Second, you draw her attention to key literary patterns. Next, you help her to do things that will stimulate physical or emotional responses. Then, just as before, you go through the whole process whenever the opportunity naturally presents itself.

The suggestions in this chapter require you to sing or recite or read aloud from literature. In case you have any doubts about your credentials for working with "literature," I can assure you that you need not be concerned. Your working materials will be lullabies, nursery rhymes, picture books, and folktales, many of which you yourself probably enjoyed as a child. The only qualification you need at this stage in your Make-your-child-a-lifelong-reader program is interest in your child's literary development and the determination to spend a minimum of fifteen minutes every day of your child's early years to foster it.

Parents should read to preschool children and informally teach them about reading and writing. Reading to children, discussing stories and experiences with them, and with a light touch—helping them learn letters and words are practices that are consistently associated with eventual success in reading.
—Becoming a Nation of Readers, *report of the Commission on Reading, National Institute of Education*

The suggestions in this chapter have one overriding purpose—to help you convince your child that the formal language of books provides food for the emotions, the imagination, and the intellect that can be found no place else. A child who becomes convinced of this will become a reader.

Goal 1: Learning to Respond Physically to Literary Patterns

When you put a book in the hands of a child who has already become a reader, she will seem to retreat from the world. Aside from an occasional giggle or a change of position, the child will show little physical response to the written material. But in order for your child to reach this quiet stage where everything goes on inside the mind, you need to make sure that she first feels the language of books in a physical way.

The best thing you can do to help your child begin to experience literature is to hold her in your arms as you sing or recite a simple nursery ditty.

Young children delight in being gently rocked or having their limbs pumped rhythmically. When these extremely satisfying activities come packaged in the simple but strong patterns of a lullaby or rhyme meant specifically for them, their pleasure grows even greater. It is through just such common nursery activities that you can give your baby her first experiences with the rhythmic patterns and language forms that are typical of literature.

SUGGESTION: Rock your baby to the rhythms of lullabies and nursery rhymes.

Rhythm is one of the most powerful tools of the storyteller or poet. It is used to capture the listener or reader's attention, to convey emotion, even, at times, to carry the burden of the literary message. Even in a simple little nursery rhyme like the one that follows, the tenor of the message changes completely when the rhythmic pattern is altered:

> I had a little pony,
>   His name was Dapple Gray;
> I lent him to a lady
>   To ride a mile away.
> She whipped him, she slashed him,
>   She rode him through the mire;
> I would not lend my pony now,
>   For all the lady's hire.

When you rock your baby back and forth to a nursery rhyme like "Rock-a-bye, Baby," you're emphasizing the lullaby's rhythmic patterns, and, as the rhymer intended, you're helping your child to physically feel its ideas.

As you sing a lullaby or chant a rhyme, take your baby in your arms and rock or swing her in time to the music of the words. Or put your child on your lap and pump her arms or legs up and down as you tell the tale of Jack and Jill or Humpty Dumpty.

Almost any rhyme, poem, or song in the literature for young children will serve your purpose, but the words of Mother Goose have proven their effectiveness with children for centuries. You will find no children's material more geared to physical expression than the nursery chants of Mother Goose. "To Market, to Market," "Oh, Where Has My Little Dog Gone?" "Pussy Cat, Pussy Cat," "Sing a Song of Sixpence," "Jack and Jill," "Bobby Shafto," and "Baa! Baa! Black Sheep" are all rhymes that work well with rocking, swinging, and knee bouncing.

Don't worry if the words you are saying seem far beyond your child's understanding. It makes little difference that your baby doesn't fully understand. A baby is never too young to get a sense of a rhyme's meaning just through the feelings that the sounds and the rhythm generate—feelings that will be all the more intense because of your attention.

SUGGESTION: Physically demonstrate the dramatic patterns of nursery rhymes and stories.

When my own children were very young, my husband's aunt would regularly entertain them by reciting a little rhyme in Russian that she had learned as a child. As she chanted the words, she rhythmically tapped the children's tiny palms. As she approached the end, her voice would rise with excitement and her fingers would race up their arms. Both the verse and the fingers ended with a wild tickle in the bend of their elbows, at which point both the children and the tickler would double up with laughter. It didn't matter that neither Aunt Dora nor the children knew what the words of the rhyme actually said; everybody got the essence of the message.

Like Aunt Dora, when you come to dramatic moments in a lullaby or a rhyme or story, let your motions accentuate them. Change the scope, the pace, or the intensity of your movement.

You can emphasize the dramatic buildup of events through any simple rhyme or lullaby. Even "Rock-a-bye, Baby" can sensitize your child to literary forms if you make a contrast between the gentle rocking motion of the baby and the threatened fall.

The most common nursery rhymes, like "This Little Piggy" and "Rock-a-bye, Baby," we all know how to do. But a parent who puts her mind to it can think of ways to physicalize other nursery rhymes.

SUGGESTION: Help your child to make the movements that are indicated in the text.

It won't be long before you will begin to notice that your baby is making little bouncing movements in concert with your words. When that happens, show her that you are pleased. Then help your baby to "dance" on her own; a nod, a smile, or an assisting hand is all the encouragement needed.

It doesn't matter if your child's movements don't really exactly correspond to the words. What does matter is that she is physically responding to the rhythm.

Before much longer your child will also begin to anticipate motions you have added for dramatic emphasis as you sing or tell rhymes and stories. If you have frequently flung her arms open, as in playing "Pat-a-cake," when you recited, "and throw it in the oven for baby and me," you will begin to note that your baby starts to tense up when you reach the crucial part. You'll feel a little pressure on your hands as she prepares to make the gesture.

These are exactly the responses you want to encourage. They mean your child is reacting personally to the words you are saying.

Before long, your baby won't need you to guide her through the motions. A reminder through your touch or in the inviting tone of your voice will ensure her participation.

Goal 2: Learning to Respond Visually to Rhymes and Stories

You have seen how you can help your child to experience the bodily sensations evoked by literature. Now you need to include another aspect of response—the visual—in your literary program.

As soon as your baby is able to focus on your words as you speak to her, it is time to help her begin to experience literature through her eyes.

The best material with which to start your child's visual experience is the literature that you've already helped your baby to feel, the lullabies and rhymes of the nursery.

SUGGESTION: Help your child to visualize characters and events by using illustrated rhymes and lullabies.

The process couldn't be simpler.

First, put your child on your lap and prop up the book so that she can see it. Then draw her attention to the book by pointing to the illustration that accompanies the ditty and identifying the major figure in it. If your rhyme is "Rock-a-bye, Baby," take your baby's hand and help her point to the baby in the illustration. At the beginning, don't overload your baby with too many things on which to focus. Wait until later to add the cradle and the tree.

Finally, ask your baby to say the name of the main character or object in the illustration as she points to it. If you want, you can help her pat the figure on the page or, if the story is about animals, make the sounds that the animals make. Do anything playful and natural that will complement the reading and focus your child's attention on the book.

It is vital at this point that you be especially sensitive to your child's level of interest. As long as you have your child's attention, continue reading. But the moment that attention flags, call a halt, even if you are in the middle of a story. Be sure to break off in a positive fashion, however.

A simple statement, such as "Let's finish this tomorrow" or "That's all for now," will keep "story time" a time that you can both enjoy. A hug or a tickle or a bounce on the knee will do much to end things on an intimate and positive note.

SUGGESTION: Read stories that direct your child to do things.

Books that give children directions to follow provide a simple kind of literary experience that both captivates your child and helps her make the link between the written message and herself. A very simple book, like Dorothy Kunhardt's *Pat the Bunny,* a book that despite its age is still going strong, is a perfect starter book.

You can enrich the experience by assisting your baby to make the movements that the words suggest. If you are reading *Pat the Bunny,* for example, take your baby's tiny fingernail and move it back and forth over the sandpaper surface that represents Daddy's beard. Or put her hand on the bunny and guide it to make patting motions.

You will soon discover, as I did with my own children, that before long, all you will need to do is put your baby on your lap and hold the book so that she can see it. Then read the words. Your youngster will follow the directions without your assistance. Give your baby ample time to look at each detail of the illustration and to respond fully.

SUGGESTION: Choose simple, well-illustrated books.

Simplicity is the keynote in choosing starter books for your baby or toddler's read-aloud program. For her first experiences with stories or rhymes (or whatever), select a book that has a simple format. There are countless books of Mother Goose to choose from, but most of them come in anthology form, presenting the whole of Mother Goose in a few pages. You might as well have the rhymes on the head of a pin for all the good they will do your baby in that form.

Find a book that distributes one rhyme or one story along several well-illustrated pages. If your baby is to "read" the book with you, text *and* illustration need to stand out boldly. For your preschooler, you need to keep the text bold, but you can relax a bit on the simplicity of the illustration. Your three-year-old will be capable of dealing with more complex and subtle visual material. For a listing of other starter books for the very young refer to the Suggested Reading section at the end of Part One.

A word of caution: Good illustrated picture books—even those intended for infants—can be very costly. But you needn't let that deter you in your quest for a book that will suit your baby or toddler's needs. At your public library, you'll find a wealth of high-quality picture books, and they will cost you nothing.

If you want to purchase the books but at a lower price than you'll find in the children's bookstores, try used book stores or thrift shops. Even prize winners like the Randolph Caldecott Medal books can be found on these shelves simply because their owners have outgrown them. If you chance upon a Caldecott Medal winner, pounce on it. These books —one each year—have been singled out as the most distinguished picture books published in the United States. You can get several of them at a used book or thrift shop for the price of one in a regular book store. Also, watch for your public library's book sale. Every so often public libraries sell off duplicates and older stock to make way for new books. The cost to you of a good children's book can be as little as twenty-five cents.

You will do well to hold onto these books, even when

your child apparently no longer is interested in them. There'll still be a day when she will enjoy them again. We grow out of things and then go back to them, particularly as children.

Goal 3: Learning to Respond Emotionally to Literature

When you say to your baby, "You're such a good baby," and she coos with pleasure, your child is not just deciphering your words, she is listening to your tone, watching the intensity of your gaze, and reading the feelings registered on your face. When she puts all this information together, several things become apparent: she is being praised for something; she is special; and she is loved.

When your child sees these same pleasurable words in a book, they have been completely stripped of their emotional tenor. Your loving gaze, your caressing sounds, and the rhythm of your words have all been removed. All that remains are five flat words on a page.

In order for your child to read those words and understand their full meaning, she will have to put back what has been stripped away—namely, their emotional component.

You don't have to teach your child how to do this; it's a natural part of her language processing equipment. But there are two things you do have to do. The first is to make your child aware of the emotional elements of written language. The second is to stimulate her emotional reaction to the people, places, and actions told of in stories, rhymes, and poems.

You can do this by the simple process of dramatic reading.

SUGGESTION: **As you read, use your voice, facial expressions, and body movements to illustrate feelings.**

Most young children are not very sensitive to the emotional content of writing. It is only when they are helped to become aware of the implied feelings and thoughts that enrich even the simplest of children's literary fare that they can become readers.

When you read to your child, you want her to feel the same emotions that the characters in a rhyme or story or other piece of literature feel. The best way to help your child make this association between written ideas and her own personal feelings is to make it dramatically clear, when you read, exactly what those feelings are.

Suppose you are reading "Little Jack Horner." The rhyme doesn't tell us what Jack experiences during this episode. In fact, the words are truly flat until we pump a little of our own knowledge of the world and people into them. Only when we supply our notions of Jack's cockiness, pride, arrogance, or surprise does the rhyme come alive. When you dramatize your reading, you're interpreting for children what they are not yet sophisticated enough to glean from the words themselves.

Even when you're reading the simplest of nursery rhymes, it's important to use your voice, your facial expressions, and your body movements to cue your child to what the central character feels. If the rhyme is "Little Jack Horner," a low, pompous tone to your voice, a thrusting out of your chest and a wagging of your shoulders will amply depict Jack's state of mind as he pulls the prize plum out of his Christmas pie.

Don't worry about the quality of your dramatic skills when you dramatize children's literature: The hammier you are, the better your child will like it—and the more likely she will be later on to participate in the drama.

SUGGESTION: Encourage your child to dramatize stories, rhymes, and poems.

As you dramatize your reading, you stir up your child's own responses. You won't have to read a rhyme, story, or poem many times before your child will start to act out the ideas along with you. After two or three recitations you will begin to notice your little "Jack" thrusting out her chest and wagging her shoulders as you say the words, "What a good boy am I."

This is precisely what you want to happen. It is through this kind of response that children learn to draw upon their own personal experiences to plump up the flat words they see on the page.

Remember that your child will still need some indication from you that her efforts please you. Some gesture of approval—a smile, a hug, or a word of encouragement ("That's great")—is all that is needed to stimulate your fledgling reader's dramatic efforts.

SUGGESTION: **Tell your children stories. Encourage other adults, especially grandparents, to do the same.**

Telling children stories is one more device to help them associate their feelings with those of literary characters. Stories that include your child in the framework of the story do an especially good job of clarifying a character's attitudes and reactions and stirring up the young listener's response.

If you have a grandparent who is a good storyteller, you have a treasure. For several years, starting when my children were one and two years old, my father-in-law regularly told them stories. Every time he was with them he had a new adventure to tell, and so they would pester him until he finally agreed that it was story time. Then the three of them would make their way to the bedroom. Grandpa Alex would sit upright on the edge of the bed; the children would lie on their stomachs with their heads propped up on their hands and their eyes large with anticipation. The three of them would emerge a half hour or so later holding hands and looking pleased as punch.

Though the plots of Grandpa's stories were always new, the characters were always the same. They were a small boy named Jeff and a small girl named Linden.

Grandpa Alex had the wisdom to make his grandchildren part of the story. And they had the good fortune to experience a character's thoughts, feelings, and attitudes firsthand.

If you are the storyteller and you need ideas for story content, use the newspapers and television as sources. With a little embroidery on a factual news item or a slight modification of a TV episode, you can create very personal stories in which your family and pets play key roles, or you can turn an ordinary family situation into an outrageous tale that has family members and pets doing impossible things.

You can also take your stories from books. Select a folk or fairy tale, read it to yourself two or three times, then tell your child the story in your own voice. You do not need to remember every detail of the story, but it is important to present a logical sequence of events and to make the connections between events that occur. You will lose the dramatic impact of the story you are telling if have to go back to add crucial details or explain why the heroine's actions caused her predicament.

The impact of your storytelling on your child will make your efforts well worthwhile. By telling your child stories, you will make her feel special. Her response to the content then becomes almost automatic.

SUGGESTION: **Encourage your child to respond vocally to dramatic moments in stories.**

For dozens of years, an old-fashioned melodrama called *The Drunkard* has been playing on the Los Angeles stage. It has endured all this time, not because of its literary merit but because people like participating in the ritual that goes along with melodrama. When the villain comes on stage, the audience hisses him. When the heroine is threatened, they moan sympathetically. When the two lovers eventually come together, the spectators sigh with ecstasy. Everybody, spectators and actors alike, is involved in the drama. They all vent their emotions, and they all have a good time.

You can give your child the same good feeling of involvement with stories and rhymes if you encourage her to respond broadly to their dramatic, emotional moments.

You will have to demonstrate this kind of response at first. You can do this as you read by stopping at critical moments and embellishing them with the appropriate oohs or ahs. After you have dramatized a story in this manner for a few readings, your child will be anxious to orchestrate it with you. When this occurs, invite your child to join the chorus. Using a free arm, conduct her responses with broad, melodramatic gestures. When you come to places where deep or painful emotions are expressed, string out the response—sustain the feeling. For lighter, dramatic moments, make your gestures short and rapid. Your child will quickly get into the spirit of the ritual and will soon be responding without your help to the emotional meaning of the story.

SUGGESTION: Provide your child with a tape or record player and recordings of books, nursery and holiday songs, and musical stories.

Once your child is old enough you can vastly expand her opportunity to experience literature in a very personal way, and to reproduce it as well, by giving her access to a record player and some inexpensive recordings of children's stories and poems. You will find dramatic readings of many of your child's own favorite nursery rhymes and stories. Often these will have been set to music, which makes them especially compelling to young children.

Recorded stories that are dramatically recited and interspersed with songs and music that underscore the events of the plot and intensify the emotional content of the story entrance young children. Give your child recordings of such classics as "Peter and the Wolf" and "Hansel and Gretel," and chances are she will play them hundreds of times. She will probably sing or dance along with the music. She may sometimes put on a record, then turn her attention to her blocks or other toys; yet you will find that every so often, she will join with the record to echo a phrase or sing a tune.

When your child experiences literature in this way—listening to it when she wants, responding physically when compelled by rhythm, responding emotionally when stirred by an event—her experience becomes completely personal. For a listing of stories and songs on records refer to the Suggested Reading section at the end of Part One.

We've discussed how by engaging your child physically and emotionally with literary structures, you can help develop her responsiveness to literature.

Now let's see how by using virtually the same techniques, you can develop still another aspect of literary response, the intellectual.

CHAPTER FOUR

Learning Predictable Literary Forms

> Little Red Riding Hood was my first love. I felt that
> if I could have married Little Red Riding Hood, I should
> have known perfect bliss.
>
> —Charles Dickens

IN STUDY AFTER STUDY, there is one thing that stands out in the
development of readers: *Children whose parents read aloud
to them are more likely to become readers than those whose
parents do not.*

Why?

Conventional wisdom says it's purely and simply a matter of the child's increased motivation. Certainly motivation
plays a part, but something else happens when you read
aloud, something that has a far greater impact on your
child's reading development.

By reading aloud you offer your child the opportunity to
learn about the language of poetry and prose—its words, its
structures, its ideas. Each pattern of sound, of structure, of
social relationship your child assimilates as you read will
make the task of learning to read that much easier, and
thereby make reading itself that much more enjoyable.

Learning to make sense out of a written language is a

process of relating the new to something already known. When your child is able to relate words or ideas to something with which he is already familiar, learning is spontaneous and the results satisfying. If he has no knowledge on which to build, attempts to learn to read are tedious and fruitless.

Hearing you read stories helps your child develop expectations about language as well as content. The knowledge of what to expect, and the excitement of surprise if the expectation is not realized, not only enables your child to better understand and appreciate what he reads, it enables him actually to decipher the words on the page with greater ease. To understand why, let's go back to household words.

Unless they are familiar with the language and also the general content of what they are expected to read, [children] experience great difficulty in reading. Certainly there will be no enjoyment. The only way to acquire a starting familiarity with the written language of various kinds of literature is to have heard it read aloud. Just as children cannot learn to read and learn subject matter at the same time—one of them must be a base for learning the other—so students will not learn how to read and enjoy literature if they are unfamiliar with the language and conventions of the literature they are trying to read. Learning always involves relating the new to something that is known already.
—*Frank Smith,* Essays into Literacy

Long before your child learned to read words like *Cheerios,* he knew what they said. You had helped him become aware that this word was on the face of the box and to expect that every time he saw the box, it would "say," "Cheerios." This expectation made it possible for your youngster to practice reading—and eventually to learn—the word.

Without prior knowledge of what to expect, either of household words or words from a story or poem, your child would be forced to read letter by letter, word by word. Instead of looking for meaning, all his attention would have to be focused on decoding, and the results would be almost guaranteed unsatisfactory.

If you have ever used one of those toy decoders that enables you to decipher a secret message, no doubt you will recall that you had to write down each letter as you decoded it. That was the only way you could remember what you had done. And even though you had deliberately and systematically deciphered each letter, you probably only made sense of the message when you got to the end and then reread it as a whole. If you were to read in the same manner, you would soon decide that reading is a tedious and unrewarding affair.

It *is* possible for a child who has no prior knowledge on which to rely to decipher text letter by letter or word by word. But given the nature of our mental processes, by the time he finally reaches the end of a sentence, he will have forgotten the beginning. Despite all their efforts, the message for word-by-word and letter-by-letter readers remains incomprehensible. There is simply too much information to process, and it takes too much time. Both these conditions thwart these readers' efforts to make sense out of a text, and children who don't make sense out of what they read soon decide that reading is simply not worth the effort.

Fortunately, your child was born with an extremely efficient language processing system, one that enables him to understand language without going through the laborious and unproductive process of considering each sound he hears or analyzing each letter or word he sees. It is a system that uses whatever information he possesses about language patterns and structures and about himself and the world to reduce the amount of information he needs to decipher to a manageable level.

To give you an idea of how this process works, think about doing a crossword puzzle. You need a word to fill a certain space. First, you narrow down the possibilities by looking at your cues—the meaning, the length of the word, perhaps a stray letter. On the basis of these cues, you make a guess about the word and enter it in the allotted space. Now you have to find out if the word you have decided upon fits in the context of the words around it. If you later find that it doesn't, you try another. Only when the whole block of words fits together are you satisfied that your decisions were correct.

Instead of trying to slog through thickets of meaningless letters and words in the fond hope that eventually some nugget of comprehension will arise, the reader is looking for meaning all the time. If any possibility of meaning is to be found in a text, the predicting reader is the one who will find it.

—*Frank Smith*, Essays into Literacy

It is now generally accepted by reading theorists that we make sense out of what we read in exactly this way. We use text cues and our knowledge of language and literature to make predictions about what words, sentences, or whole blocks of text can and cannot mean. As we read along, we check out our predictions to make sure they make sense in the context of neighboring words and ideas.

Your child learns to read text by following exactly this process. He draws upon personal knowledge to predict what might be appropriate in the literary context with which he is dealing. Simultaneously, he checks to see if the prediction makes sense.

To make your child a reader, you need to make it possible for him to discover literary patterns and to build a repertoire of expectations about literary language and content, just as you did for household words. It is this, more than anything else, that will make the difference between your child's loving and incorporating reading into his life or shunning it.

Your job is easy! It simply requires reading aloud.

Read some nursery rhymes or poems to your child. Chances are that before you have finished, he will be saying the final words in the lines.

Efficient reading does not result from precise perception and identification of all elements but from skill in selecting the fewest, most productive cues necessary to produce guesses which are right the first time. The ability to anticipate that which has not been seen is vital in reading, just as the ability to anticipate what has not yet been heard is vital in listening.

—Kenneth S. Goodman, "Reading: a Psycholinguistic Guessing Game"

Then try some folktales. It won't take many folktale sessions before your youngster, upon hearing a few paragraphs, will start to tell how Henny Penny will greet each new member of her entourage or what Little Red Riding Hood will say to the wolf.

A few fairy tales and your child will soon come to recognize simple character types—the good and virtuous heroine and the mean and spiteful villain, for example. And he will quickly come to know what fate lies in store for a fairy tale princess or a mythical ogre.

When your child hears a story or poem read aloud, he notes the conventions of form and content that guide its development. He uses this knowledge to predict how a line of dialogue spoken by Henny Penny will be resolved or what the appearance of the wicked fairy at Sleeping Beauty's birthday celebration portends. True, he may not hit upon the exact word to complete the rhyme or predict exactly the form that the fairy's revenge will take, but just having some sense of what is to come will substantially reduce the amount of graphic information he has to attend to as he reads.

The guidelines in the following sections will help you to develop a read-aloud program that will expose your child to basic literary patterns and offer you some ideas—ways of sharing what you yourself already know—for building your child's intellectual responses to simple literary forms.

If you're in doubt about what is suitable for your child's age level, call the children's department of your local library. The librarian will be able to give you some suggestions about what works at what age and level of development.

You don't have to do all the reading yourself. An older sibling can function very well in this capacity. In many communities, children's organizations, such as the Girl Scouts, offer parents their services as readers. If you are interested, ask for information at your local public library.

Let me reemphasize that you don't have to be an avid reader to make literature meaningful for your child. Nor do you have to be knowledgeable about literature. Just read aloud and share in your child's discovery.

Goal 1: Developing Expectations about Literary Language Patterns

Literature relies heavily on sound for its effect. Listen to the sound of this old-timer as you read it aloud: "Rain, rain, go away Come again, another day Little Johnny wants to play." Like in a piece of music, the sounds of this little rhyme are repeated over and over. Its words march along in careful order, the sounds dictating rhythm and pace. This simple nursery ditty is a perfect example of a language pattern that is a staple of literature.

The easiest way for you to familiarize your child with the use of such sound devices in literature is to read your child exactly this kind of material, the little rhymes and folktales of the nursery.

When you choose material for your read-aloud program, you need to look for writing that, just as in "Rain, rain, go away," depends heavily either on repetition of sound or on subtle sound transformations for its effects.

SUGGESTION: Read nursery rhymes that feature repetition of sound.

To initiate your read-aloud program, try the Mother Goose tales. With the exception, perhaps, of rhymes that require a British accent for proper resolution of sound patterns, almost any of the rhymes will help your child develop a sense of how sound is used in literature. For a listing of illustrated rhymes and lullabies refer to the Suggested Reading section at the end of Part One.

You might want to read a few rhymes out loud just to see what they sound like before reading them to your child. But that really isn't necessary: A quick scanning is probably all you will need to identify rhymes that have a subject your child would be interested in and that exhibit obvious rhymes and repetitions of sounds. This is all that is necessary to involve your child in helping you as you read.

Just as you did in getting your child to respond physically and emotionally to literary patterns, encourage your child to look at the book with you. Then as you read, let him supply words from the sound patterns that you leave out; just pause and indicate by your expression that it is your child's turn, and he will promptly do the rest.

One caution: Be careful not to overdo rhymes in any one session of your read-aloud program. A few at a time will suffice. When your child begins to squirm or fret or show other signs of loss of interest, you'll know it's time to stop reading.

SUGGESTION: Read nonsense poetry.

You can supplement your program of nursery rhymes with poetry that exhibits obvious sound patterns. But you need to exercise a bit more care in your selection: In most collections of children's poetry, the language and thoughts are simply too sophisticated for very young children.

> *Language, sound, and combinations of sounds are a source of playful exploration for children. They invent languages, collect words they delight in, make up words, and give names to objects. They laugh at the tricks their own speech plays upon them. "Look, Dad," a small child calls across the summer lawn, "I'm turning somersaults. In winter will I turn wintersaults?"*
>
> *For children, nonsense is a confirmation of experience, a language peculiarly their own, and the laughter it provokes is the most genuine mirth of childhood.*
>
> *—Edna Johnson et al.,* Anthology of Children's Literature

For starters, look for fun poems, poems that play on words and ideas. Listen to the sound patterns of these lines from Lewis Carroll's *Alice's Adventures in Wonderland* as you read them aloud:

> The Owl and the Pussy-cat went to sea
> In a beautiful pea-green boat:
> They took some honey and plenty of money
> Wrapped up in a five-pound note.

And listen to these contemporary rhymes:

> Boa Constrictor
> Oh, I'm being eaten
> By a boa constrictor,
> A boa constrictor,
> A boa constrictor,
> I'm being eaten by a boa constrictor,
> And I don't like it—one bit.
> Well, what do you know?
> It's nibblin' my toe.
> Oh, gee,
> It's up to my knee.
> Oh my,
> It's up to my thigh.
> Oh, fiddle,

It's up to my middle.
Oh, heck,
It's up to my neck.
Oh, dread,
It's up mmmmmmmmmmmmffffffffff . . .
    —Shel Silverstein,
    Where the Sidewalk Ends

The Eel
I don't mind eels
Except as meals
And the way they feels
    —Ogden Nash, *Family Reunion*

Such nonsense poetry, with its wit and its richness of sound, will tickle your child as it familiarizes him or her with the use of sound in literature. For a listing of other nonsense literature refer to the Suggested Reading section at the end of Part One.

SUGGESTION: Read folktales that feature repetition of words and ideas.

For story material, you can't beat the traditional folktales. The story of the three little pigs with its unforgettable lines—"I'll huff, and I'll puff, and I'll blow your house in" and "by the hair of my chinny, chin, chin"—provides everything you want in the way of repetitive sound patterns.

There are scores of folktales in which speeches and descriptive phrases are repeated over and over again. There are scores of others in which ideas are presented and then slightly changed with each subsequent presentation. In the tale of Henny Penny's mission to tell the king that the "sky is a-falling," there are minor changes in the pattern of dialogue as each new character enters the scene. You will want to give your child the experience of discovering and assimilating both of these kinds of patterns.

SUGGESTION: **Accentuate distinctive language patterns with your voice.**

The distinctive patterns that are repeated over and over again in the course of a story or poem help to accentuate the effect of an event or reinforce some aspect of character. They help the child to understand a story or poem, and they give him a great deal of pleasure. No matter how many times they hear "and he huffed and he puffed and he blew the house down," children never fail to respond.

Your child will assimilate these patterns and respond, too, providing you draw his attention to the key passages. For a listing of picture storybooks for reading aloud to preschoolers refer to the Suggested Reading section at the end of Part One.

When your child was younger and you were helping him respond emotionally, it was sufficient for you simply to put drama and feeling into your voice in order to excite him to the content of what you were saying. When he reaches three or four years of age, you will still be reading dramatically but with a more subtle objective in mind—to teach him to use sound patterns as cues to the meaning of stories and poems.

As you read, quickly note the key patterns. Often a pattern will take the form of a series of words that occur several times in a story, like the "Trip, trap! Trip, trap! Trip, trap!" that sounds as each of the Billy Goats Gruff crosses the ugly troll's bridge. Sometimes it will be a speech like that of Snow White's infamous stepmother: "Mirror, mirror, on the wall, who's the fairest one of all?" At other times a pattern will take the form of a repeated phrase: "Dame, get up and bake your pies, bake your pies, bake your pies . . ."

When you come upon such a pattern as you read to your child, make it stand out. Take your time as you read the key words. Draw them out. Change your tone of voice. A "Trip, trap" that marks the small goat's passage could be high pitched and quickly paced; the "Trip, trap" for the middle-size goat, heavier and slower, and that for the large goat, positively royal in tone and pace. In that way you can be sure that your child's attention will be drawn to the repeated pattern. For a listing of repetitive folktales refer to the Suggested Reading section at the end of Part One.

If you have an older child—one between the ages of eight and thirteen—ask him to read to his younger sibling. Most children of this age like to read to younger children and generally are very good at injecting drama into the activity. Both of your children will benefit. Your younger child will be motivated to read because his big brother reads, and your older child will, in the need to dramatize the material, become a more sensitive reader.

SUGGESTION: Encourage your child to say familiar parts of rhymes and folktales as you read aloud.

After a few repetitions of a language pattern, stop when you reach the key words and let your child supply them for you. The more experience your child gets in echoing or supplying the missing patterns, the more natural the patterns will seem.

As a tale grows more familiar, let your child provide the key speech or phrase all by himself. Start such participatory reading around the age of three and continue it at least until your child is six. It will prompt him to seek out literary patterns and anticipate their use in text when he reads on his own.

SUGGESTION: Encourage your child to sing nursery songs.

When children sing the words to nursery rhymes or other songs, they are using literary language. In the process they grow more and more familiar with both literary structures and literary ideas.

Singing sessions are perfect vehicles for encouraging the use of literary language. You can initiate one by simply pulling your child upon your knee and starting to sing. If you happen to have a piano or a guitar, that will make the song-fest even more appealing. For a listing of nursery rhymes and lullabies set to music refer to the Suggested Reading section at the end of Part One.

Do make a big show of important sound patterns. Make them louder or softer than the rest of the words, or let your child be the soloist in key places.

SUGGESTION: Develop your child's sensitivity to sound patterns by misreading, so that your child can catch the "mistake."

When a child is completely familiar with the rhyme pattern or oft-repeated phrase, you can have a little fun. Children love to catch you out when you're reading. Try ending a rhyme with the wrong sound or inserting a mismatched phrase in a series of repetitive phrases, and your child's ears will immediately perk up. If he doesn't correct you, you can correct yourself in an amused manner.

Let your child know that you made a mistake and that you would welcome his corrections. Actually, what you are welcoming is your child's intellectual involvement with literary language.

There is an additional benefit to be gained from such an activity. Your child will learn that mistakes aren't fatal. You want your child to risk making mistakes when he reads. If he feels he has to verify every letter and word as he reads along, reading will soon cease to interest him. With a more relaxed attitude, he can read more efficiently and quickly. If he makes mistakes, he will correct himself as he goes along.

Goal 2: Developing Expectations about Content

The behavior patterns that appear in literature are as important for your child to discover and assimilate as the language patterns that you have just considered.

To become a fluent and appreciative reader, your child needs to be able to anticipate or predict what will happen in stories—what kinds of things a character will say or do, how he or she will react, what the effect of an act will be.

Reading is a process in which information from the text and the knowledge possessed by the reader act together to produce meaning. Good readers skillfully integrate information in the text with what they already know.
—Becoming a Nation of Readers, *Report of the Commission on Reading, National Institute of Education*

The best way to help your child develop expectations about content is to read the traditional tales, legends, and myths. In the traditional oral literature, people (or, often, animals with human characteristics) are either good or evil, humble or arrogant, rich or poor, stupid or clever. And all these types behave in established modes.

It is characteristic of fairy tales to state an existential dilemma briefly and pointedly. This permits the child to come to grips with the problem in its most essential form, while a more complex plot would confuse matters for him. The fairy tale simplifies all situations. Its figures are clearly drawn, and details, unless very important, are eliminated. All characters are typical rather than unique.
—*Bruno Bettelheim*, The Uses of Enchantment

You will rarely find an in-between, ambiguous character to confuse or puzzle your child. Fairy tale and mythical characters are like your youngster's paper dolls—they are always one-dimensional, and your child can easily understand them. It is exactly because of that that they make such excellent starter characters for your child's early literary experience.

SUGGESTION: **Develop your child's expectations about the behavior of characters by reading fairy tales, legends, and myths.**

As your child hears or reads the traditional tales, he will steadily build a network of expectations about what his culture values, what its social conventions are, and how people relate to one another. Suppose you have read stories to him about foxes. Later when he sees the words "The fox ran down the road," he will be able to tap into what he knows about the physical characteristics of foxes: They are four-footed animals. They are not too large. They have pointed noses and bushy tails. The words may suggest other ideas to him also. Foxes steal chickens. They are crafty. They are not to be trusted. These are cultural ideas transmitted over the centuries through stories. This is knowledge that will enable him to understand the cultural implications that reside within the simple words he reads. For a listing of folktales in picture book form refer to the Suggested Reading section at the end of Part One.

The stories [children] hear help them to acquire expectations about what the world is like—its vocabulary and syntax as well as its people and places. . . . And though they will eventually learn that some of this world is only fiction, it is specific characters and specific events which will be rejected; the recurrent patterns of values, the stable expectations about the roles and relationships which are part of their culture, will remain. It is these underlying patterns, not the witches and giants which give them their concrete form, which make stories an important agent of socialization, one of many modes through which the young are taught the values and standards of their elders.
—Arthur N. Applebee, The Child's Concept of Story

Since the characters in ancient tales are so clearly drawn, you have only to select your stories and read. Just make sure that your selection includes a broad range of character types and that you read your tales with all the mystery, awe, and excitement in your voice that you can muster.

Your child, even if he is very young, will quickly learn

how an evil giant or a wicked stepmother will behave and what the probable consequences of their behavior will be. This is knowledge of cultural values and standards on which he can draw when he learns to read.

As you read, be sure to listen to your child. His comments or questions might indicate that he has taken in all of the story he is able to for the moment—in which case you need to bring the story session to a halt. Or his remarks may reveal that he has heard something in the story that he can't understand or doesn't relate to. Questions about why a character acted in a certain way are common among children. If your child should ask you why the queen wanted Snow White killed, it's important for you to take the time to enhance his understanding. You can answer him directly, or you can turn the question back to him to consider. When children ask questions they often are not looking for answers as much as they are for an opportunity to talk about something that is puzzling or disquieting. By being attentive to your child's remarks, you can accelerate the development of his knowledge of the world and his command of language. Both will help him to become a better reader.

SUGGESTION: Develop your child's response to character by rereading stories.

When you first read a story to your child you are taking him into a world that he has probably never encountered before. The story introduces him to new, often strange types of people, to situations that are far different from those of the everyday world, and, frequently, to ways of saying things that he has never heard before. While the story may appeal to your child, neither its situations nor characters will be sufficiently familiar to elicit his full response. It is only through successive readings that the characters in a story take on their full personalities, the settings become familiar, and the words sound natural.

Your child doesn't want—and doesn't need—a constant

stream of different stories. He needs, rather, to have the opportunity to become thoroughly familiar with a few, well-chosen stories—familiar enough to feel that the characters are like old friends, to anticipate their behavior, and to experience vicariously the perils and joys that these friends communicate.

Coming back again and again to a story will deepen your child's understanding and appreciation of the behavior of these characters, and it will provide him with a solid base of knowledge upon which to draw as he begins to read independently.

SUGGESTION: Encourage your child to tell you stories.

As children become better acquainted with stories, they begin to tell you stories. Though they are very primitive, the stories of two- and three-year-olds still reflect the content and structures of literature. Studies of children's use of story language have shown that as children—even two-year-olds —tell their stories, they play with patterns of sounds and repetitions of ideas. They often start with "Once upon a time" and end with ". . . and they all lived happily ever after." The creations of five-year-olds are almost always peopled by characters right out of fairy tales. Those of six-year-olds reveal firm expectations about those characters. The giant is "evil," the stepmother is "wicked," the fox is "crafty." What they have begun to assimilate of literary patterns and structures is surfacing. This is exactly what you want.

To get your child to use what he has learned about literary language and ideas, encourage the retelling of bits and pieces of favorite stories or rhymes.

A natural way for you to stimulate story retelling is to stop at critical points in a familiar story and ask, "What do you suppose happened then?" When your child finishes telling you, you need to acknowledge the response. Then, with a "Well, let's see," proceed with the reading.

A child's sense of story includes expectations about the behavior of various characters. . . . Story characters are the beginning of what we might call the child's "literary" or "cultural" heritage, though the child does not recognize them as such; they are reference points which children share with one another and with the world of adults. A child who plays the part of a story character, for example, is taking up a role whose possibilities have been defined by the story, and all the children involved will understand, in an unconscious way, what those possibilities entail. This sort of assimilation extends even to linguistic structures which the child would otherwise find unnatural.
—Arthur N. Applebee, The Child's Concept of Story

Remember, this is not an instructional session. This is a sharing session—a mutual enterprise.

To keep your child's participation in this enterprise, you need to accept whatever your child tells you. It is absolutely critical that you refrain from pointing out faulty renditions. Your child is telling you the things that excited his imagination or seemed funny or sad to him. He is not on trial.

If your young partner doesn't remember exactly what happened to a character, or if he drastically alters the sequence of events, don't make an issue of it. You can clear up misunderstandings or help your child to become aware of details as you reread the story or talk about it at a later time.

SUGGESTION: Accept your child's version of a story.

If you choose to reread a story, be sure to imbue the rereading with the same spirit of mutual discovery that characterized first readings. You can keep alive that sense of discovery by interjecting such comments as "Can you believe that happened?" or "Wow, that was a close call." Such comments will show your child that reading is an active intellectual enterprise that involves you, just as much as it involves him.

Suggestion: Help your child to write stories.

Children, even three- and four-year-olds, like to write stories as well as tell them. When they see their words go down on a piece of paper, they become totally absorbed. When the finished product is read back to them, they simply beam with pleasure. And along with all this pleasure comes a strengthening of their sense of story language and story structure.

You can help your youngster create stories by suggesting that the two of you write a story. Put your child on your knee—or the two of you lie on your bellies on the floor—and place a blank piece of paper in front of you. Then ask that universal writer's question, "What shall we write about?"

At first you will need to do a lot of guiding. A good way to get the story going is to decide upon a character. Who is he? What is he like? Chances are your child will want to write about someone much like himself.

By asking leading questions you can channel the structure of the story your child is creating: "Where does this take place?" "Tell me about it." "What happened then?" "And then?" "And then?" And simply write down your child's responses. Show your own response to the plot as it develops: "Oh, my goodness. What a terrible pickle. How can he get out of that?"

When the story is finished, present it to your child and let him "read" it with you.

So let's tote up where we are.

In the last two chapters, you've seen how by using literature selectively and by drawing your child's attention to basic literary patterns, you can help develop his physical, emotional, and intellectual involvement with literature. The development of these three types of responses is critical in making your child a reader.

Your efforts to assist your child's literary development will be greatly enhanced if you help him, at the same time, to value reading, to think of it as an important part of his everyday life.

In the next chapter we'll consider what you can do to make your child know that reading fills a special niche in his life.

CHAPTER FIVE

Learning to Value Reading

> "I cannot remember a time when I was not in love
> with [books]—with the books themselves, cover and
> binding and the paper they were printed on, with their
> smell and their weight and with their possession in my
> arms, captured and carried off to myself. Still illiterate,
> I was ready for them, committed to all the reading I
> could give them.
>
> —Eudora Welty, *One Writer's Beginnings*

HELPING YOUR CHILD TO BECOME A LIFELONG READER is like building a fire. First you lay the groundwork with simple written words. Then you add simple literary designs. Finally you add a variety of literary materials. At each step you attempt to expand both your child's reading experience and the range of her response. And through the entire period of development, you need to give her the kind of support that will nurture and increase her desire to read.

During the first six years of your child's life, you are the chief source of her enthusiasm for becoming a reader. It is your influence that will cause your child to make reading an accepted part of her life and to view herself as a reader. How you can use your influence will be specified in this chapter. First, however, a note on the nature of that influence.

A young expectant mother recently told me that she

was afraid her newborn baby would never become a reader. Her reason: Though she herself was a reader, her husband was not. He read things at work, but he never read at home. He simply preferred doing other things.

The young woman believed, like so many parents and teachers I have come into contact with over the years, that children become readers mainly because they see the people they care most about—their parents—reading.

It is true that children, especially young ones, are anxious to be just like their parents. This is a major tool that we, as parents, have in shaping our children's development, but it has its limitations. Indeed, for you to expect your child to become a reader just from seeing you read is wishful thinking. Seeing you read will no more turn your child into a reader than seeing you eat peas with gusto will turn your child into a pea eater. Nor, conversely, will failure to see you read prevent your child from becoming a reader.

Only the personal discovery that reading is a compelling and satisfying activity will cause your child to value reading and make it a part of her life. And in making that happen you have an active role to play.

Goal 1: Incorporating Reading into Your Life Together

When little Sarah, our young friend from Bear Valley, was ten months old, her mother and father started to read books to her. Sarah soon learned that there was a double pleasure to be had in reading. The first was one she got from the books themselves. The sounds of the words, the characters, and the adventures captivated her. She wanted her books read again and again so she could relive the feelings that each brought.

The second pleasure was one she got from being with her parents. She liked their attention and their closeness— and their praise whenever she "read" by herself. It made reading times some of the most pleasant moments of her day.

Sarah's parents demonstrated in many concrete ways that they valued her involvement with books. But they displayed their interest most powerfully by taking time to read to her, not once but several times a day. As a result, books became an indispensable part of tiny Sarah's life.

SUGGESTION: **Schedule a particular time each day for reading with your child. Regularity counts.**

For your program to be effective, reading with your child has to be more than a once-in-a-while occurrence. It must be a scheduled event that takes place every single day of your child's life, from the time she is able to attend to simple nursery rhymes until she has become an independent and dedicated reader.

You may want to build a reading program of many impromptu story sessions during the day, as Sarah's parents did. It is absolutely essential, however, that in addition to these informal times you reserve one particular story time each day that your child can count on.

Many parents find that even when their children are preschoolers, that special story time—the one that always occurs no matter how busy or chaotic the day has been—works best at bedtime. As they grow, the content of these story times may evolve from lullabies and nursery rhymes to simple picture books, then to folktales to adventures. Yet the time reserved for books always remains the same.

When you make that one very special time a part of your youngster's going-to-bed routine, you will probably find, as other parents have, that your youngster will be far more receptive to bedtime. The knowledge that she will have not only your undivided attention but a story experience as well makes going to bed much more pleasant.

Story time needs to be an oasis of quiet, of intimacy, of shared experience—a time that your child can look forward to. Therefore, it's important to schedule your reading for a time when you don't feel rushed. You need to allow enough time for the story as well as for the rituals that, if your preschooler is like most, she will impose on the proceedings —and still be able to project an attitude throughout that says to your child, "This is the most important thing we could be doing right now."

If bedtime doesn't work well in your family routine, schedule your child's story time for after dinner or before an afternoon nap. It doesn't really matter when you read with your child, as long as you do it with regularity.

SUGGESTION: Arrange alternate story times or stand-in readers for emergencies.

Even with the best of intentions, other things will inevitably intrude upon your time and you will be unable to read with your child at the reserved time. When this happens, you need to have a back-up plan.

If you know you're not going to be on hand for after-dinner or before-bedtime reading, squeeze in a story earlier in the day. It helps to warn the child ahead of the change in schedule. Or if need be, have someone else—the babysitter, a grandparent, or an older child—read with your child. However you choose to arrange it, make sure that your child has a daily reading experience. If you want to show that you value her reading, you need to honor that reading time, no matter what.

Goal 2: Identify Your Child's Interests and Match Them to Books

If you have more than one child, you have probably noted differences in their reading tastes. Not even the most carefully chosen story will interest every listener.

As early as a few months of age, children's tastes vary. Later on, when they have had a chance to hear you read to them from an assortment of materials, the variance increases considerably. It is not unusual in a first grade classroom to see one child hanging on every word when the story is about horses, while a neighboring child doodles and waits impatiently for tales of heroic deeds.

At the end of each part, various types of literary material for you to use in developing different aspects of your child's literary understanding and response are suggested. Though you may follow those general guidelines without problems, when you choose particular rhymes, poems, or stories for your child, it is imperative that you select materials that reflect your youngster's own taste. By personalizing your child's reading program, you will keep her interested and involved in reading.

SUGGESTION: **Be alert to your child's interests. Provide reading material to match.**

Before your child is old enough to tell you what she wants to read, you need to watch for her reactions—not just to the songs, rhymes, and stories you share, but to everyday situations as well. If your child perks up every time a dog appears on the TV screen or in the street in front of your house, you can bet that she will be responsive to stories about dogs.

As your child grows older, listen to her, talk to her, and observe. Pick up what excites your youngster when she plays or watches television. And then make sure she encounters plenty of written material in those areas.

Another way to ensure that your child's interests are taken into account in the selection of reading material is to allow her to select the stories to be read or the books to be borrowed or purchased.

"What shall we read today?" is a question that invites your youngster to run through her literary repertoire and find exactly the thing that suits her mood at that moment. No matter what you think of the choice, the story chosen will be right for your child, and the very fact that you have allowed her to make that choice will affirm her interest in the material itself.

Sometimes, if a preschooler's choices are too limited, she will choose any story at all, and the benefits of self-selection will be lost. This problem is easily resolved by a trip to your local library or children's bookstore for a new book. Again, let your child decide which book to take.

You may find when the selection is made that your child has decided upon a book she already has at home. Booksellers and librarians have found that it is common for children under the age of six to head immediately for an old favorite and hand it expectantly to their parents. Instead of borrowing or buying the book your child has chosen, use it as an indicator of your child's interests. Find other books with the same characters, by the same author, or on the same subject. Show them to your child, tell her how they are like the one that was chosen, and suggest that she make another choice.

While you are at the library or bookstore, take time to browse through the materials that are displayed. Make a note of the books that attract your child's attention and suggest those as candidates for future selections.

Goal 3: Developing Your Child's Image of Herself as a Reader

Your child may be a long way from being a reader, but the more you help her to feel like a reader, the more likely she will be to remain involved with books. You saw when your child was very young the pleasure she got from reciting the words beneath the pictures of her favorite storybooks. She may not have been reading, but that didn't matter; she was experiencing the feeling of *being a reader*.

The primary method of enhancing and capitalizing on that feeling is to encourage your child actually to read and to accept her efforts uncritically. I have made several suggestions about how to do that in the preceding chapters and will not repeat them here. There are still other ways, though, for you to help your child feel like a true member of the reading society.

SUGGESTION: Present books as gifts.

A concrete way to show your child that you think of her as a reader and that you value her interest in books is to make the presentation of a book part of every gift-giving event.

If you select carefully—making sure your gift is something your child will enjoy—she will probably demand that the holiday or birthday ritual include time for reading the new book.

Our family photo album testifies to our children's insistence that we stop everything and read the books that Santa Claus left. Every Christmas morning, no matter where we are (Connecticut, Brazil, New York, France), the photo is the same: There we all are, sitting amid a clutter of torn gift wrapping, tattered ribbons, and shiny new toys —with a book propped up in front of us as we gather together to share a new story. The only change in the scene over the years is in the size and shape of the books. At first they are thin and tall—one is even in the shape of a Santa. Each year they grow a little thicker and more conventional in shape.

When the children became independent readers, the Christmas morning story times disappeared. They preferred to squirrel their books away to read by themselves some time later on Christmas day. Nevertheless, our family custom of exchanging books has remained unaltered to this day.

SUGGESTION: Give your child books as little surprises.

The unexpected gift book—the one you give to your child just because you saw it and thought it would please her —comes with an even greater emotional charge than the anticipated holiday gift.

> *There's nothing wrong with telling a child, if we don't like a book or get tired of reading it, that we don't want to read it. He will enjoy our reading more if we read something that we like, as well as he. As a matter of fact, since we will probably be asked to read aloud any book that we get for a child, we would do well to make sure that we like most of these before we get them.*
>
> —*John Holt,* How Children Learn

When you choose this kind of special gift, keep your child's responses in mind. Make sure that there is something about the book that will make it especially appealing. Your thoughtfulness both in giving the book and in making sure it is of special interest makes it a gift your child will value.

SUGGESTION: **Involve your child in literary clubs and activities.**

Your child's participation in any kind of event that pertains to books, from autographing parties at the children's bookstore to book sales at the public library, will give her the feeling that she belongs to the reading world.

One of the best ways to make your child a part of the reading society is to take her to the regular story sessions that are offered by public libraries and children's bookstores. These events are typically a source of literary magic. The storytellers or readers are usually well-trained professionals with a flair for drama and an intimate knowledge of what makes children respond. And of course, the material to which they have access includes the finest of everything, from the classics to contemporary selections. Often, especially in bookstores, the material read is available for the children to borrow or purchase.

In both libraries and bookstores, the story hours are open to the public and are free. All you need to do is call for the schedule.

Go with your child at first. It will benefit you both. Your presence will shore up her confidence in the new situation, and you'll pick up some pointers on how to tell or read a story in an interesting manner. And you'll both have something to share later on.

You can also make your child feel like a reader by enrolling her in readers' book clubs. Some clubs will bring a book in the mail each month. Others—usually those offered in bookstores—make book buying tempting by giving discounts or free books after a certain number of purchases. Magazine subscriptions have the same effect as the book clubs; they make the child feel that she is a member of a select group and give her a sense of her own importance. For a listing of magazine and book clubs for preschoolers refer to the Suggested Reading section at the end of Part One.

Your child is nearing six now, and the first stage of your mission to make your child a lifelong reader is almost finished. So let's take stock of what you have accomplished.

Chances are your child is able to read many of the words she sees around the house and neighborhood, the words that identify things in her daily life. By this time she may even be able to read some or all of the words in oft-read stories. These accomplishments are, at this stage, of secondary importance, however. What is of prime importance for your child's future as a lifelong reader is that reading occupies an important place in her life.

When you read with your child, what does she do? She laughs over a numskull's ineptness; she feels sad or sorry for an ill-fated storybook character; she taps out the rhythm of a rhyme or poem; she talks about things that happen in stories, or she plays in her fantasies with storybook friends. Your child accepts both the language of literature and the unseen worlds that it describes. She finds reading to be a satisfying way of experiencing life. As a result of all this, your child has come to expect and desire that reading should be a regular part of her life.

The fire that you have so tenderly and patiently fanned has burst into flame. Your job now is to keep that flame burning brightly. To do this, you need to ensure that both your child's reading competence and her confidence in her ability to read continue to thrive.

Suggested Reading and Listening from Infancy to Age Six

ALPHABET BOOKS TO CAPTURE THE IMAGINATION

When your child shows some knowledge of the alphabet, he will be ready for these more stimulating alphabet books.

The ABC Bunny, by Wanda Gag. New York: Putnam Publishing Group, 1978.

Alphabet Discovery, by Louise W. McConkey. Great Neck: Todd and Honeywell, 1985.

Alphabet Fun, by Roger Hargreaves. Los Angeles: Price, Stern, Sloan Publishers, 1982.

Animal ABC, by Celestino Piatti. New York: Atheneum Publishing Co., 1966.

Anno's Alphabet: An Adventure in Imagination, by Mitsumasa Anno. New York: Harper and Row, 1975.

Ape in the Cape: An Alphabet of Odd Animals, by Fritz Eichenberg. New York: Harcourt Brace Jovanovich, 1973.

Bruno Munari's ABC, by Bruno Munari. New York: Putnam Publishing Group, 1982.

Hosie's Alphabet, by Leonard Baskin et al. New York: Viking Press, 1972.

Peter Piper's Alphabet, by Marcia Brown. New York: Charles Scribner's Sons, 1959.

STARTER BOOKS FOR THE VERY YOUNG

Guidelines for Choosing Starter Books

1. Look for clear and forceful illustrations and typeface.

2. Look for subject matter to which your child can relate.

3. Look for text and illustrations that elicit physical or emotional responses.

Alfie Gets in First, by Shirley Hughes. New York: Lothrop, Lee and Shepard Books, 1981.

Animals for Me, by Lois Lenski. New York: Henry Z. Walck, 1941.

At Mary Booom's, by Aliki. New York: Penguin Books, 1978.

The Baby, by John Burningham. New York: Thomas Y. Crowell Co., 1974.

Blue Sea, by Robert Kalan. New York: Greenwillow Books, 1978.

The Bundle Book, by Ruth Kraus. New York: Harper and Row, 1951.

The Chick and the Duckling, by Vladimir Suteev. New York: Macmillan Publishing Co., 1972.

Freight Train, by Donald Crews. New York: Greenwillow Books, 1978.

Good Morning, Chick, by Mirra Ginsburg. New York: Greenwillow Books, 1978.

The Great Big Enormous Turnip, by Alexei Tolstoy. New York: Franklin Watts, 1969.

Green Eyes, by Abe Birnbaum. New York: Western Publishing Co., 1973.

Henry's Busy Day, by Rod Campbell. New York: Viking Kestrel, 1984.

Here a Chick, There a Chick, by Bruce McMillan. New York: William Morrow and Co., 1983.

Inch by Inch, by Leo Lionni. New York: Astor-Honor, 1960.

The Last Puppy, by Frank Asch. Englewood Cliffs: Prentice-Hall, 1980.

Leo the Late Bloomer, by Robert Kraus. New York: Windmill Books, 1971.

The Little Red Hen, by Paul Galdone. New York: Seabury Press, 1973.

Pat-a-Cake. Illustrated by Mary Murray. New York: Platt and Munk Publishers, 1978.

Pat the Bunny, by Dorothy Kunhardt. New York: Western Publishing Co., 1962.

The Poky Little Puppy, by Janette S. Lowrey. New York: Western Publishing Co., 1942.

Quick as a Cricket, by Audrey Wook. Sudbury: Playspaces International, 1982.

Sam's Car, by Barbro Lindgren. New York: William Morrow and Co., 1982.

The Secret Birthday Message, by Eric Carle. New York: Thomas Y. Crowell Co., 1972.

The Silver Pony, by Lynd Ward. Boston: Houghton Mifflin Co., 1973.

The Snowman, by Raymond Briggs. New York: Random House, 1978.

Snuffy, by Dick Bruna. New York: Methuen, 1975.

The Telephone Book, by Dorothy Kunhardt. New York: Western Publishing Co., 1975.

The Touch Me Book, by Pat Witte and Eve Witte. Illustrated by Harlow Rockwell. New York: Western Publishing Co., 1961.

The Truck, by Donald Crews. New York: Greenwillow Books, 1980.

The Very Hungry Caterpillar, by Eric Carle. Chicago: World Books, 1970.

Where's Spot: by Eric Hill. New York: Putnam Publishing Group, 1980.

STORIES AND SONGS ON RECORDS

A Bear Called Paddington, by Michael Bond. Caedmon Records.

Beauty and the Beast and Other Stories. Caedmon Records.

Children's Greatest Hits, by Tom Glazer. CMS Records.

Folk Songs for Young Folk, by Alan Miller. Filly World Records.

Just So Stories, by Rudyard Kipling. Caedmon Records.

Peter and the Wolf. Narrated by Leonard Bernstein. CBS Records.

Singing Holidays, by Oscar Brand. Caedmon Records.

The Sleeping Beauty, by Claire Bloom. Caedmon Records.

The Stories of Hans Christian Andersen. Walt Disney.

Tubby the Tuba, by Paul Tripp. Peter Pan Records.

ILLUSTRATED RHYMES AND LULLABIES

Guidelines for Selecting Illustrated Rhymes and Lullabies

1. Look for illustrations that reinforce the ideas in the text.

2. Look for rhymes that have strong patterns of sound and rhythm.

3. Look for subject matter to which your child will respond.

4. Look for rhymes that will elicit an emotional response.

The Big Book of Mother Goose. Illustrated by Alice Schlessinger. New York: Grosset and Dunlap, 1972.

Fee Fi Fo Fum. Illustrated by Raymond Briggs. New York: Coward McCann, 1966.

O Saw a Ship a-Sailing. Illustrated by Beni Montreson. New York: Alfred A. Knopf, 1967.

London Bridge Is Falling Down. Illustrated by Peter Spier. New York: Doubleday and Co., 1967.

Mother Goose: A Treasury of Best-Loved Rhymes. Edited by Watty Piper. New York: Platt and Munk Publishers, 1971.

Mother Goose Junior Peggy Cloth Books. Illustrated by Patricia Schories. New York: Platt and Munk Publishers, 1978.

Mother Goose; or, The Old Nursery Rhymes. Illustrated by Kate Greenaway. New York: Platt and Munk Publishers, 1972.

Mother Goose Rhymes. Illustrated by Louise Gordon. New York: Tuffy Books, 1976.

Old Mother Hubbard and Her Dog. Illustrated by Paul Galdone. New York: McGraw-Hill Book Co., 1960.

The Old Woman and Her Pig. Illustrated by Paul Galdone. New York: McGraw-Hill Book Co., 1961.

The Real Mother Goose Husky Books. Illustrated by Blanche Fisher Wright. Chicago: Rand McNally and Co., 1965.

Ring O' Roses. Illustrated by L. Leslie Brooke. New York: Frederick Warne and Co., 1923.

The Speckled Hen: A Russian Nursery Rhyme, adapted by Harve Zemach. Illustrated by Margot Zemach. New York: Holt, Rinehart and Winston, 1966.

Tom, Tom, the Piper's Son. Illustrated by Paul Galdone. New York: McGraw-Hill Book Co., 1964.

NONSENSE

Guidelines for Selecting Nonsense Poetry

1. Look for poems that play on words and ideas.

2. Look for recurring sound patterns.

3. Look for wit.

Alice's Adventures in Wonderland, by Lewis Carroll. New York: Bantam Books, 1981.

The Complete Nonsense Book, edited by Lady Strachey. New York: Dodd, Mead and Co., 1951.

The History of Simple Simon. Illustrated by Paul Galdone. New York: McGraw-Hill Book Co., 1966.

The Jumblies, and Other Nonsense Verses and *The Pelican Chorus.* Illustrated by L. Leslie Brooke. New York: Frederick Warne and Co., 1954.

Prefabulous Animals. Illustrated by Edward Ardizzone. New York: E. P. Dutton, 1960.

Sing-Song: A Nursery Rhyme Book, by Christina Rossetti. New York: Dover Publications, 1969.

Tirra Lirra: Rhymes Old and New. Illustrated by Marguerite Davis. Boston: Little, Brown and Co., 1955.

PICTURE STORYBOOKS *FOR* READING ALOUD *TO* PRESCHOOLERS

Guidelines for Choosing Picture Storybooks

1. Look for illustrations that have depth and feeling.

2. Look for stories that have drama, characterization, and an absorbing plot.

3. Look for books in which illustrations and stories work together to create emotional moods.

4. Look for strong themes.

The Amazing Bone, by William Steig. New York: Farrar, Straus and Giroux, 1976.

Angus and the Ducks, by Marjorie Flack. New York: Doubleday, 1930. Also *Angus Lost.* New York: Doubleday, 1941.

The Bear's Toothache, by David McPhail. Boston: Little, Brown and Co., 1972.

Bedtime for Frances, by Russell Hoban. Illustrated by Garth Williams. New York: Harper and Row, 1976.

Bennett Cerf's Book of Animal Riddles, by Bennett Cerf. New York: Random House, 1959.

Blueberries for Sal, by Robert McCloskey. New York: Viking Press, 1948.

Caps for Sale, by Esphyr Slobodkina. New York: Scholastic, 1976.

Corduroy, by Don Freeman. New York: Viking Press, 1968.

The Country Bunny and the Little Gold Shoes, by DuBose Heyward. Boston: Houghton Mifflin Co., 1974.

Curious George, by Hans Rey. Boston: Houghton Mifflin Co., 1973.

Emmett's Pig, by Mary Stolz. Illustrated by Garth Williams. New York: Harper and Row, 1959.

Frederick, by Leo Lionni. New York: Pantheon Books, 1966.

Frog and Toad Are Friends, by Arnold Lobel. New York: Harper and Row, 1977.

The Funny Little Woman, by Arlene Mosel. New York: E. P. Dutton, 1972.

Goodnight Moon, by Margaret Wise Brown. New York: Harper and Row, 1977.

The Great Green Turkey Creek Monster, by James Flora. New York: Atheneum Publishing Co., 1979.

Harry the Dirty Dog, by Gene Zion. Illustrated by Margaret B. Graham. New York: Harper and Row, 1976.

The House on East 88th Street, by Bernard Waber. Boston: Houghton Mifflin Co., 1975.

Ira Sleeps Over, by Bernard Waber. Boston: Houghton Mifflin Co., 1972.

The Island of the Skogg, by Steven Kellogg. New York: Dial Press, 1976.

Johnny Crow's Garden, by Leslie Brooke. New York: Frederick Warne and Co., 1903.

The Knight and the Dragon, by Thomas A. DePaola. New York: Putnam Publishing Group, 1980.

Little Blue and Little Yellow, by Leo Leonni. New York: Pantheon Books, 1963.

The Little Engine That Could, by Watty Piper. Illustrated by George Hauman and Doris Hauman. New York: Scholastic, 1979.

The Little House, by Virginia Burton. Boston: Houghton Mifflin Co., 1978.

Little Toot, by Hardie Gramatky. New York: Putnam Publishing Group, 1978.

Madeline, by Ludwig Bemelmans. New York: Viking Press, 1930.

Make Way for Ducklings, by Robert McCloskey. New York: Viking Press, 1941.

Mike Mulligan and His Steam Shovel, by Virginia Lee Burton. Boston: Houghton Mifflin Co., 1977.

Millions of Cats, by Wanda Gag. New York: Putnam Publishing Group, 1928.

Pooh's Bedtime Books, by A. A. Milne. Illustrated by Ernest H. Shepard. New York: E. P. Dutton, 1980.

The Runaway Bunny, by Margaret Wise Brown. New York: Harper and Row, 1977.

The Story about Ping, by Marjorie Flack. New York: Viking Press, 1933.

The Story of Babar, by Jean de Brunhoff. New York: Random House, 1933.

Sylvester and the Magic Pebble, by William Steig. New York: Simon and Schuster, 1969.

The Tale of Peter Rabbit, by Beatrix Potter. New York: Frederick Warne and Co., 1902.

Where the Wild Things Are, by Maurice Sendak. New York: Harper and Row, 1963.

REPETITIVE FOLKTALES

Follow the guidelines for choosing picture storybooks, page 93.

"Drakestale"	"The Knee-high Man"
"Henny Penny"	"The Old Woman and Her Pig"
"Little Red Riding Hood"	"The Pancake"
"Teeny-Tiny"	"The Talking Pot"
"The Fisherman and His Wife"	"The Three Billy-Goats-Gruff"

NURSERY RHYMES AND LULLABIES SET TO MUSIC

A Cat Came Fiddling, and Other Rhymes of Childhood. Illustrated by Irene Haas; introduction by Burl Ives. New York: Harcourt, Brace, 1956.

Cock-a-Doodle Do! Cock-a-Doodle Dandy! A New Song Book for the Newest Singers. Illustrated by Anita Lobel. New York: Harper and Row, 1966.

The Complete Nursery Song Book. Illustrated by Walt Kelly. New York: Lothrop, Lee and Shepard Books, 1954.

Frog Went a-Courtin'. Illustrated by Feodor Rojankovsky. New York: Harcourt, Brace, 1955.

Hush, Little Baby. Illustrated by Aliki. Englewood Cliffs: Prentice-Hall, 1968.

The Little Drummer Boy. Words and music by Katherine Davis, Henry Osorati, and Harry Simeone. Illustrated by Ezra Jack Keats. New York: Macmillan Publishing Co., 1968.

Lullabies and Night Songs, edited by William Engvick. Illustrated by Maurice Sendak. New York: Harper and Row, 1965.

Sing Mother Goose. Illustrated by Marjorie Torrey. New York: E. P. Dutton, 1945.

Sleep, Baby, Sleep: a Lullaby. Illustrated by Gertrud Oberhansli. New York: Atheneum Publishing Co., 1967.

This Little Pig Went to Market: Play Rhymes. Illustrated by Margery Gill. New York: Franklin Watts, 1967.

SINGLE FOLKTALES IN PICTURE BOOK FORM

Always Room for One More, by Sorche Nic Leodhas. Illustrated by Nonny Hogrogian. New York: Holt, Rinehart and Winston, 1965.

The Bremen Town Musicians. Illustrated by Paul Galdone. New York: McGraw-Hill Book Co., 1968.

Cinderella, translated from Charles Perrault; illustrated by Marcia Brown. New York: Charles Scribner's Sons, 1954.

Dick Whittington and His Cat, by Marcia Brown. New York: Charles Scribner's Sons, 1950.

The Fisherman and His Wife. Illustrated by Margot Zemach. New York: W. W. Norton, 1966.

The Fool of the World and the Flying Ship, by Arthur Ransome. Illustrated by Uri Shulevitz. New York: Farrar, Straus and Giroux, 1968.

Humpy, by P. Yershov. Illustrated by Jacqueline Ayer. New York: Harcourt, Brace and World, 1966.

Jack and the Beanstalk, by William Stobbs. New York: Delacorte, 1966.

The Original Peter Rabbit Books, by Beatrix Potter. New York: Frederick Warne and Co., 1902-1922.

Peter and the Wolf, by Serge Prokofiev. Translated by Maria Carlson. New York: Viking Press, 1982.

Puss in Boots, by Charles Perrault. Mahwah: Troll Associates, 1979.

Rapunzel, by the Brothers Grimm. New York: Harper and Row, 1975.

Rumpelstiltskin, by the Brothers Grimm. Mahwah: Troll Associates, 1979.

Salt, adapted by Harve Zemach. Illustrated by Margot Zemach. New York: Farrar, Straus and Giroux, 1977.

Seven Simeons, by Boris Artzybasheff. New York: Viking Press, 1961.

The Shoemaker and the Elves. Illustrated by Adrienne Adams. New York: Charles Scribner's Sons, 1960.

The Sleeping Beauty, by Charles Perrault. Translated and illustrated by David Walker. New York: Harper and Row, 1977.

Snow White and Rose Red, by the Brothers Grimm. Mahwah: Troll Associates, 1979.

Snow White and the Seven Dwarfs. Translated and illustrated by Wanda Gag. New York: Putnam Publishing Group, 1938.

The Story of the Three Bears. Illustrated by William Stobbs. New York: McGraw-Hill Book Co., 1964.

The Story of the Three Wise Kings, by Tomie DePaola. New York: Putnam Publishing Group, 1983.

The Three Little Pigs. Illustrated by William Pène du Bois. New York: Viking Press, 1962.

The Three Sillies, by Paul Galdone. Boston: Houghton Mifflin Co., 1981.

The Three Wishes. Illustrated by Paul Galdone. New York: McGraw-Hill Book Co., 1961.

The Wolf and the Seven Little Kids, by the Brothers Grimm. Mahwah: Troll Associates, 1979.

The titles of additional books with carefully selected recommended reading lists may be found in the Appendix.

MAGAZINES *FOR* PRESCHOOLERS

Kidstuff, Guidelines Press, 1307 S. Killian Dr., Lake Park FL, 33403.

Sesame Street Magazine, One Lincoln Plaza, New York, NY, 10023.

National Geographic World, Dept. 01185, 17th and M Sts., N. W., Washington, D. C., 20036.

BOOK CLUBS *FOR* CHILDREN *UNDER* AGE SIX
Hardcover

Grow-with-Me Book Club, Garden City, NY 11530 ($2.49 per book)

Books for the Very Young

Picture Story Books

Beginning Reader Books

Growing Readers' Books

Junior Literary Guild, Garden City, NY 11530 ($2.95 per book)

Preschool

Picture Books

Easy Reading

I Can Read Book Club, 1250 Fairwood Ave., Columbus, OH 43216 ($1.89 per book)

Parents' Magazine Read Aloud and Easy Reading Program, Box 161, Bergenfield, NJ 07621 ($1.95 per book)

Weekly Reader Children's Book Club, 1250 Fairwood Ave., Columbus, OH 43216 ($1.89 per book)

School Book Clubs: Paperback

Buddy Books Paperback Book Club, Field Publications, 4343 Equity Dr., Columbus, OH 43216 ($.70–$3.00 per book)

Club del Libro, Niño y Juveniles, AIMS International Books, Box 11496, 3216 Montana Ave., Cincinnati, OH 45211 ($.99–$6.95 per book)

Scholastic Book Clubs, 904 Sylvan Ave., Englewood Cliffs, NJ 07632 ($.35 to $.50 per book)

See-Saw Book Program

Lucky Book Club

Troll Book Clubs, 320 Rt. 17, Nahwah, NJ 07430 ($.75–$.95 per book)

Xerox Paperback Book Club, Box 1195, Education Center, Columbus, OH 43216 ($.30–$.70 per book)

Buddy Books

Goodtime Books

For more complete information on children's book clubs, see Nancy Larrick's *A Parent's Guide to Children's Reading* (Philadelphia: Westminster Press, 1982).

PART TWO

AGES SIX THROUGH ELEVEN:
Developing Competence and Confidence

CHAPTER SIX

Becoming a Self-Sufficient Reader

> It is a great thing to start life with a small number
> of really good books which are your very own.
> —Sir Arthur Conan Doyle, *Through the Magic Door*

LEARNING TO READ is much like learning to play chess. It takes very little knowledge for you to begin, but becoming accomplished takes years.

It takes just a little knowledge for children to begin to read, but that's only the beginning. To become readers they must develop their skills and gather knowledge of words, of literary forms, and of the world. The only truly effective way for them to do that is to read: To read you have to read.

> *The best way to get children to refine and extend their knowledge of letter-sound correspondences is through repeated opportunities to read.*
> —Becoming a Nation of Readers, *Report of the Commission on Reading, National Institute of Education*

So far you have whetted your child's appetite for reading and you have helped him develop enough skills to be able to do some reading. Now you need to turn your attention to making your child a self-sufficient and self-motivated reader, one who can read without help and who does it for the joy that he gets from it or, as a matter of course, for accomplishing things he wants to do.

Now that your child is in school and spending more and more hours away from home, it is no longer possible for you to always be there with the book that will excite or the words that will inspire or encourage. Even if it were possible, the nature of your role in making your child a reader would change.

This period, from ages six through eleven, is one of great growth. These are the years when children are beginning to be independent. These are the years when your child begins to show personality patterns that can make it more difficult for you to do some of the things that you might wish to accomplish. There are few babies who won't allow you to read to them or who won't play the games you want to play with them. Children in this age bracket, however, are beginning to exhibit patterns of behavior that are often contrary to those a parent would want. Sometimes there is resistance to parental guidance. What seemed natural and caring to your child of two or four is not going to be met with the same acceptance. As your child begins to give up the simplicity of his behavior, helping him become a reader becomes a little bit more of a job and less of a game. This means that there is now all the more need to deal with your child's reading development on a programmatic and conscious level.

One of the influences you have to deal with is television. TV is, in the words of noted educator Benjamin Bloom, a "thief of time." As such, it is the enemy of reading. Time spent watching television is time spent not doing anything else—and one of the things children are not doing is reading. There are probably fifty different ways you can look at this, but my view is that TV must be restricted. You need to set a limit to the amount of time your child can watch it. There shouldn't be a TV in your child's room. If he gets up early, he shouldn't have TV; he should have books, games, or toys to entertain himself. If you make this decision, you may not be popular for a while. But once the pattern is established, your child will accept it and benefit from it for the rest of his life. Reading will be his companion long after he has lost his taste for Bugs Bunny.

This is a critical period in your child's reading development. He needs your guidance and support now, more than ever, to keep his interest in reading high and to ensure that the skills and knowledge he needs to become a lifelong reader continue to develop.

Goal 1: Expanding and Capitalizing on Literary Interests

When we make literary experience a prominent part of preschoolers' lives, they come to expect that reading will be a satisfying experience, one that will stimulate the mind and arouse emotions. This expectation sometimes produces a problem, however.

Studies of children's reading interests have shown that what will satisfy six- to twelve-year-olds intellectually and emotionally are stories about life's trials. They respond particularly to stories that emphasize a mastery of those trials. In addition, children at this stage of development like to read language that is highly emotive, that makes them want to laugh or cry. And they want to read stories that stretch the imagination.

The problem is that what your child reads in school will probably not be about the things that interest him, and reading with his teacher will not be an experience like the one he has come to know at home. Instead of reading sensitively written stories and sharing the thrills the words evoke with a caring parent, he'll read a few lines of text from a story that has been developed to teach him to associate certain sounds with certain letters. His first stories will consist of a few simple words. They will have no plot and no setting. They will tell him nothing about characters. After he reads, he will answer his teacher's questions and fill in blanks on the assigned page of his workbook. Even if he perseveres and achieves, he will still not be doing the kind of reading that will give him pleasure or excite his imagination.

> *Enjoyment of a story tempts the reader to project himself into it, to anticipate the ideas to come, and to use context clues in identifying unfamiliar words. Lack of interest, on the other hand, results in listless, perfunctory reading and willingness to substitute words that do not make sense.*
> —Characters in Textbooks, *a review of the literature,*
> *United States Commission on Civil Rights*

If his only exposure to reading at this stage in his development were to be the exposure he gets at school, his expectation that reading would add something to his life will almost certainly begin to dim, and the anticipation with which he looked forward to becoming a reader will fade.

The surest way to prevent your child's school experiences from dampening his desire to become a reader is to make sure that, at least at home, your child has books to read that will satisfy him intellectually and emotionally, books that are compelling enough to keep him reading.

SUGGESTION: Start your child's independent reading program with familiar and well-liked stories.

Children learn to read more easily if they know what they are reading about. By using prior knowledge, children are able to read materials that would completely bog them down if they lacked that resource. Therefore, it is important —particularly in the early stages of learning to read without assistance—to select books for your child to read that have a familiar context.

To start an independent reading program, suggest that your child read some of the books that he liked when he was younger—the picture books or the Mother Goose tales that you read together, for example. Encourage him to read these very simple books to younger siblings. He will enjoy practicing on stories that are obstensibly too babyish for him if he can rationalize his return to baby books by reading to a younger sibling. For a listing of folk and fairytales, myths, and legends that appeal to children refer to the Suggested Reading section at the end of Part Two.

When he feels confident as a reader, add the folktales that you read to his reading list. Children who have been read folktales—as your child has, if you followed part one of this program—have a fund of literary knowledge. They know the heroes and the villains, the lost child, the donors and the helpers. And they know how these characters will behave. They know about magic charms, and they expect them to help the hero perform difficult tasks and defeat his foes. In addition, they are familiar with the sounds and patterns of the language used. They expect stories to start with "Once upon a time" and end with, "And they all lived happily ever after." This knowledge makes it possible for them to build their reading skills as they read stories that have some substance and are motivating.

If you select a folktale your child already knows and likes, he will automatically apply all past knowledge about folktales, knowledge that you helped him gather. Your novice reader may not be able to figure out all the words—and you will need to help sometimes—but he will be able to achieve satisfying results nonetheless. Of course, not all children find folk and fairy tales to their liking. Many prefer to read about characters that are "real." You can honor that preference and still select stories and books that meet your criterion of familiarity if you give your child books to read that are part of a series.

Series like The Hardy Boys and The Bobbsey Twins have endured for decades because young readers find them both easy to read and stimulating. Though each story in a series is different, they are like folk or fairy tales in that they are written to formula. The specifics differ, but the characters, plots, and language patterns conform to a preset design. Children quickly come to discern the patterns and apply them as they read through a series. By the time your child has read through two dozen Hardy Boys books, interest in the series may begin to flag. But by then, his reading skills will have improved sufficiently to allow satisfying reading of other types of books. For a listing of books with sequels refer to the Suggested Reading section at the end of Part Two.

SUGGESTION: **Encourage your child to read interactive stories.**

A completely different kind of story that your child will probably find captivating enough to keep him going, even if reading itself is a struggle, is the multiple-ending adventure story. This is a relatively new and extremely popular type of children's fiction. The stories are constructed so that the reader guides their development. The completion of the story requires the reader to make decisions in crucial moments in the plot. The reader is given a series of options and chooses the one that appeals most. He then reads along a particular line of plot resolution (he may then go back and choose another). These stories are particularly helpful in encouraging young readers not just to rely on the words in the text for meaning but to put some of their own understandings into stories. Perhaps more important, these stories are fun! Your youngster will want to read them.

SUGGESTION: **Borrow books and magazines from the library.**

Once you have found the right formula of book for your child, stay with it. You need not worry that the only thing your child will ever learn to read is *The Hardy Boys*. At a certain point, he will have had enough and will turn to other things.

At the same time you want to extend your child's reading horizons and vary the reading diet. The easiest and least expensive way to do this is to borrow books and magazines from the public library. For a listing of magazines for ages six to twelve refer to the Suggested Reading section at the end of Part Two.

A library can be an overwhelming place for a young child, and you need to help him feel comfortable and secure there. It's important to allow plenty of time for the first visit.

Getting a first library card is a special moment. You can heighten your child's feeling of pride at being a member of the library by explaining what the card entitles him to do and the procedures for its use. Getting him a book bag for carrying his treasures home will also enhance the feeling that this is a special event in his life.

After you get your child his library card, introduce yourselves to the librarian in the children's section and ask to be shown around. Then take some time for just the two of you to browse through the shelves. Read some of the titles and talk about them. When you chance upon a story that your child knows and likes, bring it to his attention and talk about the things he most liked about it. Then see if you can find other books by the same author. If you do, leaf through them and read a line or a passage here and there. Or better still, let your child read whatever catches his eye.

When you have an overview and know which shelves hold the books you are interested in, have your child pick out a few that he finds appealing. Take time to sit down at a table and look through these tentative choices together before you make your final selections.

SUGGESTION: **Build a library at home.**

Though children find the act of reading independently thrilling enough to want to read more, everything you can do to enhance and endorse their involvement with books intensifies the experience and boosts their self-esteem as readers.

> *Respond to what the child is trying to do. The motivation and direction of learning to read can only come from the child.*
>
> —*Frank Smith*, Essays into Literacy

Two simple ways to show your child that you recognize his new reading status are to make a place for his own books and to buy book plates to identify the books as his own.

One of the best ways to fill that bookshelf—and to extend your child's literary horizons at the same time—is to have your child join one of the children's book clubs. Each month a number of first-class publishers offer children mail-order books at minimal prices. For as little as thirty-five cents your child can buy the finest of children's literature in paperback. All by itself, that monthly book can rapidly expand your child's literary repertoire. For a listing of book clubs for ages six to twelve refer to the Suggested Reading section at the end of Part Two.

You might also want to open a charge account in your child's name at a bookstore that has a good selection of children's books and let your child select a book on a regular basis. Or you can go with him to thrift shops, used book stores, and garage sales to find treasures.

Don't forget to look for treasures that may be beyond your child's current reading competencies. Your child's response to literature still needs developing, and his mind and his imagination need stretching. He needs to read for himself, but he also still needs to be read to. The pleasure of being read to can last a lifetime. It's not just the six- to twelve-year-old who enjoys listening while someone reads; it's the sixty-year-old as well. For a listing of books for ages six to twelve that contain heroes, heroines, and thrills refer to the Suggested Reading section at the end of Part Two.

Goal 2: Expanding and Capitalizing on Nonliterary Interests

Your child's interests serve as the springboard for his pursuit of learning and his development of competencies. But only your conscious effort to make life experiences and literary experiences work together for your child will broaden his range of reading interest enough to propel reading development successfully.

In this phase of your Make-your-child-a-lifelong-reader program, you need to cultivate your child's habit of using printed material to accomplish aims or to make life more interesting. This habit, perhaps more than anything else, will develop your child's reading interests and, at the same time, develop his reading skills.

SUGGESTION: Expand your child's literary and life interests through family outings.

One of the most natural ways to broaden children's reading range and to develop their reading competency is to involve them in seeing or doing things that will arouse their curiosity—then to make sure that they have access to books or any other printed materials that will satisfy their need to know.

You can foster this synergism between real life and books by going with your child on outings and by using print to extend and enhance the experience.

If you live in an urban center, your family outing might take the form of a visit to the zoo. There the experiential possibilities abound. Imagine putting your child face to face with a kangaroo. Then imagine sharing with him what knowledge you have of kangaroos in general and of this kangaroo in particular. Part of the information you share is printed on the placard in front of the cage—the kangaroo's vital statistics. You might then recall what you have read in the newspaper about this kangaroo's birth or his sale to this zoo. You also share any information you have on the kangaroo's homeland. By the time you are ready to move on to the next cage, your child's knowledge of this animal and of the world in general has been enhanced immeasurably, and so have his interests.

And if your child follows the typical pattern, he will pursue that interest by seeking out books on kangaroos.

In addition to zoos, urban locations offer museums of all sorts, children's theaters, parks, festivals, and special events. Whichever you choose for your weekend outing, it will help your child to develop.

If you live in a nonurban area, your outings will most likely take the form of nature hikes. These can be as valuable, if not more so, than a visit to a museum. An overnight camping trip can develop your child's interests in a dozen different directions. If you point out things that interest you as you go along, you'll open your child's eyes to the world around him and stimulate his curiosity. He will want to know about the animals, plants, and rock formations you encounter. He will want to know about the history of the area. And he'll want to know practical things, too! How to set up camp or read weather signs or identify stars and planets or mix the batter for pancakes. Share what you know with your child. What you don't know you can read about together.

Get your child to become the family "expert" by looking things up in advance of a trip. His interest in outings and receptivity to new experience will definitely be enhanced when he becomes involved in the planning of the event.

Even if your child's reading skills are too feeble to do the job, encourage him to look at any reading material you might have and to join in on the discussion about how to spend the afternoon.

SUGGESTION: Encourage your child to develop hobbies.

Another good way to help your child reach out for knowledge and experience is to encourage his interest in hobbies.

It doesn't matter what it is, any hobby carries with it a whole new realm of experience.

Listen attentively when your child talks about what his good friends are doing, and you will probably get clues to your child's own interests. Or watch for interests as your child responds to TV commercials or programs. Then just ask if he wouldn't like to start a garden or build a windmill or make a simple calculator. If the answer is yes, go out together to collect the information and the materials that will make the project possible.

Even if you know where to go, what to get, and how to do it, your first stop should be the public library. Look through the children's books and magazines that tell about your project. Then select one that gives the details about materials and how to proceed in simple language. Now you are ready to gather up the things you need to get your project going.

You will help your youngster to build a much more enduring interest if you and your child collect the various requirements for your hobby and assemble them yourselves, but this can be a time-consuming project. If that's a problem, you may be able to find a hobby kit that will do just what you want and thus avoid the trouble of going from place to place to assemble your materials.

As your child's interests mature and his reading skills develop, you will want to expand into the practical realm of the how-to book. Choosing suitable books, once again, is simply a matter of asking yourself what it is that your child cares about, then finding a book to match that interest.

In some cases your quest for the right book will be easy. If your child spends most of his spare time playing soccer, you will have no difficulty finding books at an appropriate level. Beginning, intermediate, and advanced books on soccer plays, techniques, and stars abound. If your child is a stamp buff, however, it might be a little harder for you to find books that are written at your child's level of interest and understanding.

Your best source is the librarian in the children's section of your local library. One telephone call can usually produce a list of books that will fit your needs. With one more call to your nearby bookstore you can order the book you want.

SUGGESTION: Teach your child how to use written directions.

If your child is to proceed independently with projects, he needs to know how to use written directions. Understanding directions and using them to accomplish something may seem to your child like a formidable challenge of his reading skills. But you can make it possible for him to follow written directions by teaching simple procedures for understanding and acting upon them.

One of the best ways to help your child learn to follow written directions is to get him involved in cooking. You can start cooking with your child before age six, but after age six, at this stage of his reading development, he can best learn to process cooking recipes. For a listing of cookbooks for ages six to twelve refer to the Suggested Reading section at the end of Part Two.

The first thing the two of you will want to do is read the ingredients. If your child's reading vocabulary is not up to the task, you read the list aloud, leaving time in between each item named to allow your child to go to the cupboard or refrigerator to get it.

When all of the ingredients have been located, focus your child's attention once more on the cookbook. Now you want to read all of the steps in the recipe. Let your child attempt the actual reading, but you should help with difficult words. Then, like food advisers on radio and television, repeat the instructions. When the recipe has been thoroughly understood, have your child read and follow each direction, taking one step at a time. When the preparations are finished, review each step with your child.

As soon as your child is able to read recipes, buy a children's cookbook and let him cook alone or with friends.

Other activities that will engage your child in reading and following directions are crafts and sewing and building models. Science projects are also good if your child shows interest.

Be sure as you introduce each new type of activity that you provide your child with the amount of assistance required to follow the directions. And be sure to take a look at the directions before your child tries to follow them to ascertain their frustration potential. If *you* can't follow them, the chances are your child won't be able to either—but not always.

Furthermore, give your child a chance to help you if you are doing something that involves following written directions. Let him read the instructions to you or help you to figure them out, just as you are helping him.

SUGGESTION: Use TV to spark literary and life interests.

If used judiciously, your TV can be a very good reading stimulus for your child. Both programs for adults and those for children have the potential to pique interest in finding out more about a subject or a person through reading. Dramatized versions of children's literature can motivate your child to read other books by the same author or books with similar characters or plots. To make television work to assist rather than defeat your efforts to make your child a lifelong reader, there are three guidelines to follow:

First, you must choose programs with care. To select programs that will stimulate your child's interests, you would do well to seek the advice of one of the agencies dedicated to upgrading children's television. These TV watchdogs evaluate programs that might be of interest to children and put out reports on their findings. They make evaluations on the basis of how well programs are crafted, how honest they are, and how respectful of children's intelligence. Their recommendations can guide you to presentations that will engage, stimulate and challenge your child—qualities TV programs must have if they are to assist your reading program. All of these agencies put out newsletters. They will put you on their mailing lists if you request.

The TV Watchdogs: Sources for Help in Selecting Television Programs to Stimulate Your Reading Program

National Council for Children and Television, 20 Nassau St., Suite 200, Princeton, NJ 08542

Action for Children's Television, 46 Austin St., Newtonville, MA 02160

National Telemedia Council, 120 E. Wilson St., Madison, WI 53703

Citizens' Action for Better Television, 1629 Locust St., Philadelphia, PA 19103

The Radio/Television Council of Greater Cleveland, 1219 Rhodes Tower, Cleveland, OH 44115

You can use the critics' guidelines to help you make your own decisions about TV programs that will enhance your reading program. You won't have the advantage of previewing specific programs as TV critics do, but you can tell by watching one program in a series whether the series is up to your standards.

Dramatized versions of good books and stories, such as "Faerie Tale Theatre" and "Little House on the Prairie," can do much to stimulate your child's interest in reading—providing you follow up TV viewing with materials in print. A fourth-grader with a deep interest in nature and a dislike for reading became an ardent reader of *Little House on the Prairie* and its sequels when he learned from watching its dramatization on TV that the book contained a wealth of information on natural science.

Second, you must watch TV with your child. You can only be aware of the interests that a TV program stimulates in your child if you are aware of his reactions. The remarks your child makes about the contents of the program and the thoughts and feelings that seeing it generates will alert you to potential reading interests.

Third, you must make sure that your child has time to explore in print the stories or subjects that impressed him as he watched TV. If his reading time is usurped by television viewing, the TV-reading connection will be forfeited.

To keep young people reading,

Surround them with materials within their spectrum of reading.

Ensure that they read within a supportive, nonthreatening situation.

Give them time to read.

Make it possible for them to share their reading experience.

Make sure that subject matter is readily available.

—G. Robert Carlsen, Books and the Teenage Reader: A Guide for Teachers, Libraries, and Parents

---

You might do well to turn to the discussion on television (pp. 167–170) for ages twelve and older, because a lot that is said there might also apply to the six- to twelve-year-old. This material will give you a fuller vision of the possible uses of TV in your reading program.

The years between six and twelve mark the flowering of children's reading skills and their belief in themselves as readers. Youngsters delight in their new-found independence. They want to read more, just for the joy of being able to read. But as you will see in the next chapter, these are also the years when reading changes from a private and caring interaction between them and their parents to a public performance in the classroom. And the change comes at a time when they are most vulnerable to self-criticism and self-consciousness.

You have been instrumental in bringing your child to the point of independence. Now you must help your youngster surmount this personal dilemma. The suggestions in the next chapter will show you how.

CHAPTER SEVEN

Linking Private Knowledge to the Printed Message

He ate and drank the precious Words—
His Spirit grew robust—
He knew no more that he was poor,
Nor that his frame was Dust—
He danced along the dingy Days
And this Request of Wings
Was but a Book—What Liberty
A loosened spirit brings—

—Emily Dickinson

IMAGINE THIS SCENE. It takes place in thousands of classrooms at about ten o'clock every morning.

The teacher calls for the first reading group—the blue jays—to come to the reading circle. The better readers—the robins and the eagles—take out their workbooks and prepare to do their seatwork assignments. The jays come to the front of the room. Their faces are shiny. They are alert and responsive. Then they open their books and begin to read.

There is suddenly a change. Gone are the bright looks, the gregarious exchanges, the alert responses. They stumble in their reading, laboring over each word. When asked a question, they hesitate and look down as though searching among the words for the proper response.

Finally an answer comes, but it shows little knowledge of the relationships between the ideas, objects, people, and events about which they have been reading. Their minds seem to have been put on hold. Only when reading time is up and the books are closed do the jays come to life again.

It doesn't matter that the children are bright. It doesn't matter that the words they have tried and failed to read are words that they speak every day. It doesn't matter that the episodes portrayed concern people and events that are well within their range of experience. They still don't understand what they are reading.

The difference in the response of the blue jays from that of the robins and eagles, who are average and better readers, is a difference in their confidence to meet the demands imposed upon them in reading instruction.

What children feel about their competence to deal with anything, whether playing a sport or cooking a pie or reading a book, has a direct bearing on both the quality of their performance and their interest in pursuing the activity. When a child's intellectual confidence falters, her reading comprehension suffers, too, and so, ultimately, does her desire to read.

The inspired young reader—the child who responds to print with as much, if not more, enthusiasm than she responds to spoken language—is a child who is absolutely convinced that her personal responses to literature, whether they are physical, emotional, or intellectual, are both valid and worthwhile. And that is a result of both competence and confidence.

If you have been following the suggestions in this book, you have already done much to encourage your child's responses to literature. And because of that, her habit of relating personal experiences, feelings, and thoughts to literary situations has become well established. That is still not enough, however, to ensure success when she reads at school. During my teaching years, I frequently met with the parents of the blue jays in my classes to discuss their children's progress in reading. I was often startled to discover that the perception I had of my pupils differed so markedly from those of their parents. Often the child who was seen by her parents as outgoing, fully engaged, and confident I saw as intellectually timid, afraid to voice an opinion or venture a response to even the simplest question.

The difference in the response that I observed in school and the response the parents noted at home reflects a difference in the confidence of children to meet school demands. In the reading circle they were asked to publicly tell what stories were about, recall details, or explain how or why things happened to certain characters. This demand for public display of logic is often the last straw for young, uncertain readers.

To help your child develop the necessary competence and confidence, make sure that she is, first, familiar with the logical thinking processes that are reflected in writing and, second, at ease in employing the same processes to develop her own ideas. To accomplish this you need only to give your child practice in putting into words what she knows or thinks or believes.

Only by means of friction against other minds, by means of exchange and opposition, does thought come to be conscious of its own aims and tendencies.
—*Jean Piaget,* Judgment and Reasoning in the Child

There are two ways to help your child link private knowledge with the printed message. The first is by verbal expression, the second by written expression. In this chapter you will learn how to encourage both.

Just by fostering your child's verbal and written expression—and by showing her that you care about what she says and writes—you will build your child's competence and confidence in reading.

Goal 1: Putting Private Knowledge into Spoken Words

Children's reading competence and confidence has its roots in activities that give them the opportunity to express to a caring adult their own thoughts about things that matter to them.

Many years ago my husband and I attended a small dinner party at the home of friends. Another of the guests happened to be Bennett Cerf, the publisher and TV personality. He was also a writer of children's joke books.

It was the custom of our hosts on such occasions to feed their young children, then six and seven years old, and get them ready for bed before the guests arrived. They would allow the children to make a brief appearance to say hello before being shunted off to bed.

On that particular night, the children entered the living room with Mr. Cerf's books—all of them—in hand. The famous man promptly placed both children on his knees, propped one of the books up so they all three could see, and began to read. Every so often, as he went through one joke after another, he would stop and ask the children, "Did you really like that one? What do you think of this?" Or he'd say, "I'm not so sure this one works. I keep trying to think of a new ending for it. Can you think of one?"

The children were completely absorbed, not just because they were considering jokes that they knew and liked but because their minds and opinions were respected by an adult. The writer's attention and his invitation to them to help him make the jokes better showed the children that they had the ability to read, to think, and to express themselves. And it gave them the confidence to attempt all three.

This is exactly what you want to broadcast to your own child. You can do so by taking advantage of naturally occurring family interactions to elicit your child's expression of her own ideas, thoughts, opinions, and feelings.

SUGGESTION: Encourage your child to talk to you about things he or she has done.

When your child tells you what happened to her at the school picnic or recounts her escape from a fierce dog on the way to the park, she unconsciously structures the story in exactly the same manner as a writer structures a narrative. First comes the selection of what the storyteller believes to be the essential facts. Then comes the organization of those facts so that they make sense. Finally comes the selection of words to reflect the emotional content of the event.

Don't expect your child's accounts to be objective and well reasoned. Her stories probably won't show much awareness of what listeners expect in the way of presentation of events and logical conclusions until she is ten or eleven. She will seldom attempt to justify a chain of reasoning and will often be unaware that her conclusions are contradictory or paradoxical. In addition, she may focus on one feature of an experience and neglect other important ones.

Even though in your child's early efforts her logic may lack exactitude and objectivity, she is beginning to think logically and to use words to convey a personal perception of life. Eventually her thinking will become more logical, the language more precise. But before that can happen she needs to talk.

Young children can hardly wait to get home to tell their parents what happened to them during their time apart, so it is relatively easy to get your child to put into words the things she has done or thought or felt. Usually just an invitation to tell you about things that have happened to her will suffice.

Your child will respond delightedly to your interest,

providing you remain attentive to what she is trying to share with you. Nothing is more defeating to a child's attempts to tell an adult a story than to notice that the adult keeps moving around or that her eyes keep drifting down to the newspaper or over to the TV. If you are involved in something else or don't have time to really listen to what your child has to tell you, tell your child so. To say, "I'm right in the middle of this and I can't stop now" will be better than giving your child your divided attention. But then do set a time when you will be free: "I'll just be ten minutes" will let your child know that you really do want to hear what she has to say.

A second communication rule to remember in fostering your child's verbal explorations is one I have stated before: avoid correcting. This is definitely not the time to challenge the way she is telling the story. If you need to ask questions to help you understand, ask them with tact. Make it plain to your child that it is you who needs clarification, not her story that is inadequate. You can do that by showing your absorption in your child's story as you encourage her to restate unclear thoughts. One noncritical way to help your child express herself more clearly is to make a simple statement like, "I didn't get what happened after the teacher left the room," or "Can you tell me more about that?"

It's even more important to refrain from using your child's confidences as the basis for criticism of or punishment for something your child tells you she has either done or failed to do. By doing this, you risk cutting the lines of communication forever. A successful professional man in his fifties still remembers the feelings of hurt and injustice that he had when as a young child he would come home from school and tell his mother what had happened during the day. "She was an authoritarian who tended to take the side of the teacher," he recalls. She wanted to know what I had done wrong. It got to feel like I was on the witness stand. I would cut the story down, and I would fib. I didn't want to communicate the truth, since the truth always got some form of criticism or punishment."

There will be times when your child will tell you something that you don't want to hear, that your don't approve of, or that disappoints you. Hear your child through without interrupting with expressions of displeasure. If something has bothered you, approach it in a problem-solving manner. Let her know what's bothering you and talk it through. At the same time let her know that you appreciate her willingness to share this information with you.

The new code of communication with children is based on respect and on skill. It requires (a) that messages preserve the child's as well as the parent's self-respect; (b) that statements of understanding precede statements of advice.
—Haim G. Ginott, Between Parent and Child

Not all children are spontaneous storytellers. Some are timid; others are private. But almost all will willingly share experiences with their parents, providing their parents show interest in something specific that they care about. A perfunctory, "What happened at school today?" will probably earn you an uninformative "Nothing" or a shrug of the shoulders. When children have little interest in the question, they typically either respond with a single word or they don't respond at all. In either case they're telling you that your question is not worth considering. To avoid this kind of turnoff, you need to exercise your most adult conversational skills.

SUGGESTION: Encourage your child to talk about things that she cares about—even if you don't.

A good way to capture your child's interests and, at the same time, to sidetrack any defensive feelings that might prevent your child from sharing her experiences is to initiate the communication with specific questions about things in which you know your child has some kind of an emotional investment. Even better, direct your queries to things in which you both have an investment. If you've helped get your child's Halloween costume ready, ask your child to tell you about the events that accompanied trick-or-treating. A question like "What did the kids do when they saw your robot costume" will encourage your child to talk about the events of the evening.

SUGGESTION: Help your child to consider all aspects of an event.

When your child comes home and tells you about her meeting with that fierce dog, you can be sure that the story will include what happened and where it happened; often, however, at this age level the when, how, and why aspects of the episode will be left out, and the order of events will perhaps be jumbled.

When this happens, help your child to broaden her thinking and to develop her stories in a more orderly fashion by suggesting that you need a little more information, just so you can understand what happened.

You can accomplish both ends by guiding the storytelling in exactly the same way as when your child dictated stories to you. Questions that encourage further explanations, such as "And what happened then?," "How did the dog get out of the yard?" and "How did you manage to get away?" will help to establish order in the chronicle and make it more comprehensive.

Simple remarks, too, can help broaden your child's thoughts about the experience. A statement like "But I don't understand why Peter pushed you" or "I thought that dog was friendly" or "I wonder why he chased you" will encourage your child to look for explanations for things that are not readily apparent.

Your questions can also prompt your child to express her opinions about the dynamics of a situation. Leading questions, like "What do you suppose started the fight?" or "What else could she have done?" will lead the storyteller to go beyond the mere recital of facts and tell you what she thinks about them.

Children are sometimes reluctant to answer questions because they fear hurt or rejection. With your tone of voice or a smile, assure your child there are no right or wrong responses to your questions—that you will accept anything she says. Try to avoid arguing, cross-examining, or probing for information that may lead to punishment. This will certainly put an end to communication. It's important for you to remember your goal: to help your child gain competence and confidence in verbalizing experiences, thoughts, and feelings.

SUGGESTION: Involve your child in making decisions.

To help your child broaden her interpretive thinking, include her in talks that have some definite purpose. If your child is very young, just seek her opinion about simple things, like when to go to the supermarket or where to go and what to do on your Sunday outing. Later on involve your child in helping to make more complex decisions, ones that involve analyzing the ongoing situation and assessing alternatives. Major and minor purchases, changes of school, summer camp selections, places for family vacations are all subjects to which your child can contribute her thinking. They are also subjects in which your child has a vital interest.

The effects of your child's involvement in these family decisions will be twofold: it will give her practice in assessing the facts of a situation and reaching some conclusions, and it will give her a sense of her intellectual worth. After a certain point, reading ceases to be a decoding problem and becomes a reasoning problem. The better your child is at reasoning and the more confidence she has in her reasoning powers, the more apt she will be to become a reader.

You won't realize an effect on either competence or confidence unless you make sure that your child's opinion truly counts when decisions are finally made. I'm not suggesting that you let your child's opinions dominate your family decisions, only that if you want your child's full and continued participation, you need to weigh her thoughts with as much care as you do those of the other members of the family.

SUGGESTION: Encourage your child to evaluate stories or books that she likes.

You can begin to develop your child's habit of thinking and talking about books very early on by simply showing your child that you both want to hear and respect what she has to say.

If you are reading and your child is not otherwise occupied, you can choose material from your reading to share with her. "What do you think of this," you might ask her, or explain how you agree or disagree with the author.

Another way to show your interest and elicit your child's literary evaluations is to watch for expressions of pleasure or displeasure as she reads. When you hear a giggle or a snort, that's your cue to ask what happened. Then talk about the episode. It's as simple as that.

To get a discussion going that will stimulate your child's thinking, share your own reactions to the material that has piqued your child's interest. And then, borrowing from Mr. Cerf's example, ask the kinds of questions that will cause your child to reflect on what made the book work or not work, and what could be done to improve it.

SUGGESTION: Encourage your child to talk about story details, particularly those describing characters and settings.

When you ask children between the ages of six and eleven to tell you about a story, you can expect that between 65 and 95 percent of their comments will pertain to story action. Even when information is explicitly stated, they will rarely describe a character or tell you the character's thoughts or intentions or the relationship between two or more characters. Nor are they likely to tell you much about the locale of the story. It's even less likely that they will talk about a character's feelings, intentions, and thoughts about situations and other characters when those are not specifically mentioned in the story. This does not necessarily reveal that they haven't understood these aspects of the story; it does, rather, reveal that they have not attributed much importance to them.

You can help your child to develop a deeper understanding and appreciation of the stories she reads independently by helping her become more aware of details that describe character and place.

The easiest way to do this is to ask your child to tell you about the story she is currently reading. And then, as the events unfold, ask questions that will cause her to think about details. Couch your questions in such a way that they seem a natural product of your interest in the story. Also pose them at strategic times, when they won't stop the flow of the narrative or seem intrusive.

The best time to get your child to describe a character or place is before the story begins. "Who is this story about?" or "Where does this take place?" are inquiries that your child will accept as expressions of your interest. If the information provided is scanty, you can even make deeper probes, such as "What does she look like?" or "What kind of a place is it?" without interfering with the narrative or annoying the storyteller.

As your child tells the story, you can elicit details of a character's thoughts, intentions, or conversations by asking, "What do you suppose he thought about that?" or "I wonder why she wanted to go to the ball game?" or "What did she say when that happened?"

Your questions will help sensitize your child to structural elements that give the story depth, and they will also serve a much more critical reading purpose—that of helping your youngster to develop the habit of drawing upon her own knowledge of people, places, and situations to interpret story content.

You might want to vary the routine from time to time by suggesting that your child retell the story through hand or finger puppets. The task of creating the puppet dialog will focus her attention on characters' thoughts, feelings, motives, and intentions and sensitize her to this kind of information when she reads. You can make this activity really compelling if your child puts together a puppet theater in which to mount her dramas. *Making Easy Puppets,* by Shari Lewis (New York: E. P. Dutton, 1967), is an excellent source of information on puppet fabrication for children.

The puppet theater can also be used to mount one-man plays and mock radio shows, both of which will serve the same purpose, helping your child respond to a wider range of the information offered in stories.

Don't attempt to turn these theatricals into therapy sessions. Your presence as an appreciative audience is all your child needs. Just being there and laughing or applauding at the proper time will keep your child performing—and growing as a perceptive and interpretive reader.

Goal 2: Putting Private Knowledge into Written Form

I first became aware of how writing can contribute to making children readers some years ago when I was gathering material for an article on education for *Pageant Magazine.* It was then that I met a fourth grade teacher in a public school in New York City.

Most teachers have some special interest and talent that gives a unique shape to their programs. This teacher's interest was writing, a fact that was immediately apparent when you entered her classroom. Within weeks of the start of school, the bulletin boards of her classroom were covered with children's writings. The entire school year, aside from the occasional holidays that called for seasonal decoration, every inch of postable space in the classroom boasted a child's story, poem, report, or essay. Each week dozens of new writings replaced the old ones.

As the production mounted, so did the young writers' skills in putting what they saw or felt or thought into written form. By the end of the first semester, children who had started with six-line reports on "What I Did on My Summer Vacation" were writing poems about the wind swirling the leaves in Central Park or essays about the plight of the derelicts who frequented the benches down the middle of Broadway on New York's Upper West Side.

The fourth-graders were expressing thoughts, feelings, and opinions about themselves and the world with a clarity of thought and image and an expressive power that few adults are capable of.

A large, fat book that one of the fourth-graders showed me was particularly impressive. It contained a record of all the books each child had read independently during the school year. It was obvious that these children were prodigious readers. What was the connection between reading and writing, I wondered.

Studies of how children learn written language have provided some insights. They have shown that there is an interaction between reading and writing. When children read, they learn how to produce written language. When they write, they learn to read with greater understanding. As they put what they observe and think and feel into their own writing, they become more responsive to situations in both the real world and the worlds they read about. And more important, they become practiced at understanding the relationship between the two.

When children have the opportunity to write at the same time they learn to read, their development in both areas is enhanced.

It won't be hard for you to engage your child in writing activities. Once children have mastered writing implements and know how to spell a few words, they are eager to write.

You only need to provide a little guidance in order to get your child going.

Since your child is usually eager to do the things you do, you will want to start your writing program with some project you typically engage in, yet one that is within the scope of your youngster's interests and capabilities.

SUGGESTION: Encourage your child to write cards and letters.

If you're a letter writer, letter writing is an ideal project for your beginning writer—providing the task is scaled down so that it doesn't overwhelm. If you don't write letters, you could develop the habit yourself, and it wouldn't be bad for you!

It is best to start with writing projects that will help your child make the transition from talking about an event, feeling, or thought to writing about it. You also want to find a project that will give your child a sense of accomplishment yet not demand too much time or skill.

The best beginners' project is note writing. Writing a personal note comes closer to talking than any other writing endeavor; therefore it is a natural form for a beginning writer.

To proceed, all you have to do is suggest that your child add a note to your own letter to Grandma or whomever you might be writing that your child knows well. Your child will probably want to start writing right away. For the success of the project, however, it is important that you delay the writing until you have a chance to help your child get her thoughts organized on what to write about. Many of the frustrations your child might otherwise feel in writing will be avoided by just a little advance planning.

The first thing you can do to help your child focus her efforts is to get her to think about the recipient of the letter. You can do this by talking about Grandma and exchanging memories of times you have had together. Or you can share some of the things you plan to put in your letter, perhaps telling why you want to include them.

When the image of Grandma has been established, encourage your child to think about the content of her note. You want to be careful when you do this not to impose your own ideas upon your child's writing. Your goal is simply to help her develop some ideas of her own prior to writing.

To do this, ask general questions that will help your child think about things she has done or observed or felt or thought that would be of interest to Grandma, questions like "What are you thinking of telling Grandma?" or "What have you done this week that you think Grandma might like to know about?"

If this doesn't produce results, explore specific areas of experience with such questions as "Let's think about things that happened at school that you could tell Grandma about" or "Is there anything you want to tell Grandma about your new friend?" "About soccer?"

For your child to get both satisfaction and pleasure from writing, you need to make sure that you let her proceed independently but still provide whatever help she needs. The best way to maintain this delicate balance is to give your novice writer a piece of paper and a pencil of her own and a place to write where you can both work side by side. A kitchen table or even a couple of lap trays and side-by-side chairs will give the two of you the proximity that will make you readily available to spell words or talk some more about Grandma and the kinds of things she might like to hear, and still allow each of you to do your independent writing.

As your child gains in competence, she will no longer need nor want your immediate presence, but until she is well launched as a writer, do remain available for consultation both before and during a writing project.

A small note of caution: When your child is very young, she will be unable to wait for you to read what she has written. Like all writers, she will be anxious for approval. When the scope of her letter writing broadens to include friends and pen pals, however, your child will probably prefer to keep her writings private. Be sensitive to your child's needs for privacy. A good rule to observe—even with very young children—is to refrain from reading your child's letters until she asks you to do so.

If your child asks you to read her letters, show her that you welcome the opportunity. But be sure to respond as a confidant, not as a critic. Find something to praise in your young writer's efforts, no matter how inept they are. You can always say with all honesty, "I think Grandma will really be pleased to hear from you." If you find the spelling wrong—and it will be—or the thoughts muddled—and they will be—keep it to yourself. For this moment, just be an appreciative audience.

SUGGESTION: **Encourage your child to write greeting cards.**

Many parents, once their children's skills have developed sufficiently, stop interacting with them on letter-writing projects. Instead of treating letter writing as something that they and their children do together, they treat it as their children's obligation. It's no longer, "Let's write Grandma a letter"; it becomes, "You need to write Grandma" or "You'd better write to thank Uncle Joe for your Christmas present." Even children who start out enthusiastically to write letters will come to view the writing as distasteful when obligation—as it so often does—becomes the sole reason for writing. You will need to nurture your child's scope of letter writing before feelings that it's a distasteful obligation dim her pleasure.

One way to vary the activity is to turn it into a gift-making act—such as producing a greeting card. When youngsters in this age group create a card for a special person, they tend to focus on the recipient of the card and to choose words and sentiments that will give pleasure. They don't think of what they are doing as drawing or writing; they think of it as making a gift.

To get a greeting card project going, bring out your old greeting cards and look through them with your child. The samples will give her an idea of the form and help her to pick up some of the literary patterns—patterns of sound and sentiment—that are typical. That preview and some materials are all that your child is apt to need in order to develop her own cards.

SUGGESTION: Correspond with your child for "entertainment only" purposes.

Another way to inject a sense of something other than "duty" into letter writing is to correspond with your child about the funny things that have happened during the day or thoughts you have had that will amuse or please her. Then post the letters in unpredictable places: under the milk carton in the refrigerator, in her lunch box, in her pocket, attached to the dog's collar. When she responds, she will hide your letters in unexpected places, too.

SUGGESTION: Encourage your child to write mock letters.

Your ten- and eleven-year-old's imagination will be titillated and her sense of humor unleashed as she writes letters guaranteed not to be sent. These letters, usually addressed to companies, can take two forms. They can be complaints in which your child tells an executive how terrible the company's product really is and what horrible things have resulted from its use, or they can be testimonials that extravagantly praise.

If you make it clear that the purpose of these letters is to amuse the writer and, if she chooses, the family, her sense of the absurd will surface, and she will feel free to express it.

Nothing is as rewarding as writing a letter and getting something back. Letters that actually produce something in return enhance a child's interest in writing. Once she has experienced the receipt of a brochure or an autographed photograph or a free gift, she will be sold on letter writing.

SUGGESTION: Propose letter-writing projects that will result in your child's obtaining something he or she wants.

Suggest to your child that she write letters that will result in the receipt of something that is meaningful to her. If she is involved with the family in planning the summer vacation, propose that she write to travel agencies for brochures. If she is interested in rock stars, propose a fan letter that includes a request for a photograph. There is a wonderful book that you can find in the children's department of most bookstores called *Free Things for Kids* (Meadowlark). This book will inspire your child to write away for freebies. Be alert to your child's interests and make your suggestions as wide-ranging as possible.

Though the writing in these letters leaves little room for your child to use a variety of literary patterns or forms, don't worry. Their value lies in their motivating your child to both read and write.

SUGGESTION: Make writing notes a family custom.

When writing is a regular part of family interaction, children quickly come to think of it as a natural way to share thoughts, to amuse others, or to organize their lives.

You can add a writing dimension to your family life by making it a custom for all the members of the family to post notes about things that struck them funny, provoked a thought or question, or required communicating. Jokes, strange words, proverbs, bloopers, photographs with funny captions, even reminders to feed the cat are all capable of developing your child's habit of expressing herself in writing.

If you have the space, put up a bulletin board and reserve it for such messages. If you don't have wall space, use your refrigerator door instead. Buy several sets of magnets for family members to use to post messages.

Encourage your child to join with other members of the family in sharing bits and pieces of writing. And show her that you appreciate her contributions.

SUGGESTION: Encourage your child to write stories for younger children.

Once your child has gained some confidence in putting her thoughts into words, she will be ready to embark upon imaginative writing. Though eventually you will want to encourage exploration of many different forms, at the beginning, your child will feel most comfortable and get the most benefit from writing stories.

Before your child attempts to write a story, you need to give the project some direction. One of the first things to do is establish the tone of the story, just as you did in your letter-writing projects, by identifying the story's audience.

To get your story project going, try suggesting that your child write for a younger brother, sister, or friend. Writing for such an audience has a number of things going for it. First of all, it lightens the task. The stories for this audience can be short and simple. Second, it lightens the emotional load. This is a noncritical audience. Most of all, though, stories for wee folk fall naturally into the story forms, mainly folktale forms, that your young writer has been listening to and reading and knows best of all. Without even thinking about the project, your child is set with a beginning and an end for her story and a distinct pattern for the ideas that will come in between.

All you have left to do now is make sure that your child has some idea for a central character. Just as you talked about Grandma, discuss with your child what the imaginary person or persons in the story are like. You don't want to overdo this discussion, just prolong it enough to make sure your child has a character in mind; then let her write.

Don't expect creative genius. Your child's first story creations will probably look like nothing more than rather crudely linked together series of events. No matter. They will still say something about your youngster's personal experiences.

If the mechanics of writing pose too much trouble for your six-year-old, have her dictate her story to you. When you and your child have finished writing the story, read it back to her. Then have her read it to you.

All children will respond to the suggestion that they read their stories aloud to you. They like having an audience for their creations, and they also like having the opportunity to dramatize them with gestures and voice.

Each story your child writes will increase her facility in applying to written language her own knowledge of how and why things happen and how situations and people are related.

SUGGESTION: Have your child use a word processor for writing projects.

Many of the obstacles that make writing difficult for writers in this age group—chiefly handwriting, spelling, and revising—are completely eliminated when children write on a computer with a word processing program. With a word processor, children don't have to labor over the formation of letters or wait for someone to help them spell a word. And they never feel forced to destroy a creation just because it got off track. The computer enables them to focus on words and ideas instead of on the mechanics of writing.

If you happen to have a home computer with a word processing program, be sure to give your child the opportunity to use it for writing projects. Even if your child types with the hunt-and-peck system, any of the projects suggested above can be achieved with a word processor in much less time. That in itself will stimulate your child to write. If your child is a poor speller, a word checker or automatic spelling feature in your word processing program will do much to make writing activities enjoyable. And there may be an added bonus in the form of spelling improvement. Informal evaluations by teachers who have tried word processing programs in their classrooms indicate that writing with a word processor enhances students' knowledge of how to spell words. Yet the big bonus, as far as your child is concerned, is the professional-looking piece of writing that emerges from the printer when the work is done.

When children do not feel too constrained by requirements for correct spelling and penmanship, writing activities provide a good opportunity for them to apply and extend their knowledge of letter-sound correspondences.
—Becoming a Nation of Readers, *Report of the Commission on Reading, National Institute of Education*

You also want to suggest to your child some writing projects that take advantage of the special characteristics of the word processing programs. For a fun project that lets children play with story conventions and language patterns, have your youngster save on the computer an array of bits and pieces of plots or dialogue—anything that strikes her as funny. These are the makings of a patchwork story. By ordering the elements and tying them together with words of her own, your child will come up with a completely original, and very funny, story.

A family newsletter is also a good computer project, since it permits your child to gather and write news items as they occur and store them on the computer. Just before publication the items can easily be put into some sort of logical sequence, given headlines, and printed.

No matter what medium your child employs to express herself, the thing that will guarantee continued participation is success. A computer printout is a tangible record of success. It has the power to substantially boost your child's belief in herself as a writer.

The speaking and writing projects that you and your child have undertaken together have been geared to develop competence in the use of both oral and written language. Equally important, however, they have been designed to help your child perceive herself as a successful user of language. And a natural thing for a competent and confident language user to do is to read.

Your child is nearing twelve now, and her needs and opportunities are changing. Even though your youngster may have the highest levels of reading skill and commitment at this moment, she will soon be looking for other ways to satisfy the desires to experience and to know.

In the next phase of your program for making your child a lifelong reader, your objectives will be twofold: to help your child continue to grow as a reader and to help her continue to think of reading as a primary source of knowledge and pleasure. The suggestions that follow will help you and your child to accomplish both aims.

Suggested Reading for Ages Six Through Eleven

FOLKTALES THAT APPEAL TO AGES SIX AND SEVEN

The Elves and the Shoemaker, by the Brothers Grimm. Mahwah: Troll Associates, 1981.

The Bremen Town Musicians, by the Brothers Grimm. New York: Greenwillow Books, 1980.

Cinderella, by Marcia Brown and Charles Perrault. New York: Charles Scribner's Sons, 1954.

The Golden Goose, by the Brothers Grimm. Mahwah: Troll Associates, 1981.

Hansel and Gretel. Illustrated by Paul Galdone. New York: McGraw-Hill Book Co., 1982.

Henny Penny. Illustrated by Paul Galdone. Boston: Houghton Mifflin Co., 1968.

Jack and the Beanstalk. Illustrated by Paul Galdone. Boston: Houghton Mifflin Co., 1982.

Little Red Riding Hood. Illustrated by Paul Galdone. New York: McGraw-Hill Book Co., 1974.

The Old Woman and Her Pig. Illustrated by Paul Galdone. New York: McGraw-Hill Book Co., 1961.

The Pancake, by Anita Lobel. New York: Greenwillow Books, 1978.

The Sleeping Beauty, by the Brothers Grimm. New York: Atheneum Publishing Co., 1979.

The Story of the Three Bears, edited by W. U. Ober. Delmar: Scholars' Facsimiles and Reprints, 1981.

The Story of the Three Little Pigs. Illustrated by Joseph Jacobs. New York: Putnam Publishing Group, 1980.

The Steadfast Tin Soldier, by Hans Christian Andersen. Boston: Houghton Mifflin Co., 1981.

FOLKTALES THAT AGES EIGHT AND NINE ENJOY HEARING AND READING

Alladin and the Wonderful Lamp, in *Arabian Nights Entertainments,* by Andrew Lang. New York: Dover Publications, 1969.

Beauty and the Beast, by Gabrielle Susanne Barbot de Gallos de Villeneuve. In *The Blue Fairy Book,* edited by Andrew Lang. New York: Dover Publications, 1965.

Brer Rabbit, by Joel C. Harris. Topsfield: Merrimack Book Service, 1978.

Dick Whittington and His Cat, by Marcia Brown. New York: Charles Scribner's Sons, 1950.

East of the Sun and West of the Moon, by Kathleen and Michael Hague. New York: Harcourt Brace Jovanovich, 1980.

The Fisherman and His Wife, by the Brothers Grimm. New York: Greenwillow Books, 1979.

The Flea, by Johanna Cole. New York: William Morrow and Co., 1973.

From Tiger to Anansi, in *Anansi, the Spider Man: Jamaican Folk Tales,* by Philip M. Sherlock. New York: Thomas Y. Crowell Co., 1954.

The History of Tom Thumb, edited by Alison Lurie and Justin G. Schiller. New York: Garland Publishing, 1932.

The Knee-high Man and Other Tales, by Julius Lester. New York: Dial Press, 1972.

Mollie Whuppy, by Walter de la Mare. New York: Farrar, Straus and Giroux, 1983.

Peter and the Wolf, by Sergei Prokofiev. New York: Viking Press, 1982.

Rapunzel, by the Brothers Grimm. New York: Harper and Row, 1982.

Rumpelstiltskin, by the Brothers Grimm. Mahwah: Troll Associates, 1979.

The Three Sillies, by Paul Galdone. Boston: Houghton Mifflin Co., 1981.

The Well at the World's End, in *The Well at the World's End: Folk Tales of Scotland,* by Norah Montgomery and William Montgomery. Topsfield: Merrimack Book Service, 1980.

FOLK AND FAIRY TALES, MYTHS, AND LEGENDS FOR AGES NINE AND TEN

Guidelines for Choosing Folktales and Fairy Tales, Myths, and Legends

1. Look for stories that match your child's interests.

2. Look for authentic versions of the stories.

3. Look for dramatic action and dramatic tension in the development of the stories.

About Wise Men and Simpletons: Twelve Tales from Grimm. Translated by Elizabeth Shub; illustrated by Nonny Hogrogian. New York: Macmillan Publishing Co., 1971.

American Tall Tales, by Adrien Stoutenburg. Illustrated by Richard M. Powers. New York: Viking Press, 1966.

Chronicles of Robin Hood, by Rosemary Sutcliff. Illustrated by C. Walter Hodges. New York: Oxford University Press, 1960.

A Fair Wind for Troy, by Doris Gates. Illustrated by Charles Mikolaycak. New York: Viking Press, 1976.

The Golden Treasury of Myths and Legends, adapted by Anne Terry White. Illustrated by Alice Provensen and Martin Provensen. New York: Western Publishing Co., 1970.

The Heroes, by Charles Kingsley. Illustrated by Joan Kiddell-Monroe. New York: E. P. Dutton, 1963.

The Horn of Roland, by Jay Williams. Illustrated by Sean Morrison. New York: Thomas Y. Crowell Co., 1968.

The Iliad of Homer, edited by Barbara Leonie Picard. Illustrated by Joan Kiddell-Monroe. New York: Oxford University Press, 1980.

The Other World: Myths of the Celts, by Margaret Hodges. Illustrated by Eros Keith. New York: Farrar, Straus and Giroux, 1973.

Sir Gawain and the Green Knight, edited by J. R. R. Tolkien and E. V. Gordon. New York: Oxford University Press, 1967.

Stories of King Arthur and His Knights, edited by Barbara Leonie Picard. Illustrated by Roy Morgon. New York: Oxford University Press, 1955.

The Sword and the Grail, retold by Constance Hieatt. Illustrated by David Palladini. New York: Thomas Y. Crowell Co., 1972.

Zlateh the Goat and Other Stories, by Isaac Bashevis Singer. Illustrated by Maurice Sendak. New York: Harper and Row, 1966.

BOOKS WITH SEQUELS FOR AGES SIX TO TWELVE

Guidelines for Choosing Stories for Your Child to Read Independently

1. Look for characters and events that will arouse your child's emotions.

2. Look for emotive language.

3. Look for themes that are strong.

4. Look for dilemmas that your child might be experiencing in his or her own development.

Amelia Bedelia, by Peggy Parrish. New York: Harper and Row, 1963.

Amelia Bedelia and the Surprise Shower

Come Back, Amelia Bedelia

Play Ball, Amelia Bedelia

Adventures for Paddy Pork, by John S. Goodall. New York: Harcourt Brace Jovanovich, 1968.

Ballooning Adventure of Paddy Pork

Paddy Finds a Job

Paddy Goes Traveling

Paddy's Evening Out

Paddy's New Hat

Bedtime for Frances, by Russell Hoban. New York: Harper and Row, 1976.

A Baby Sister for Frances

Best Friends for Frances

A Birthday for Frances

Bread and Jam for Frances

The Borrowers, by Mary Norton. Illustrated by Beth and Joe Krush. New York: Harcourt Brace Jovanovich, 1955.

Borrowers Afield, 1955

Borrowers Afloat, 1973

Borrowers Aloft, 1974

Borrowers Avenged, 1982

Corduroy, by Don Freeman. New York: Viking Press, 1976.

A Pocket for Corduroy

Frog and Toad Are Friends, by Arnold Lobel. New York: Harper and Row, 1979.

Days with Frog and Toad

Frog and Toad All Year

Frog and Toad Together

Little Bear, by Else Holmelund Minarik. Illustrated by Maurice Sendak. New York: Harper and Row. 1978.

A Kiss for Little Bear

Father Bear Comes Home

Little Bear's Friend

Little Bear's Visit

Little House in the Big Woods, by Laura Ingalls Wilder. Illustrated by Garth Williams. New York: Harper and Row, 1973. Thirteen sequels.

Little Toot, by Hardie Gramatky. New York: Putnam, 1939, 1978.

Little Toot on the Grand Canal

Little Toot on the Mississippi

Little Toot on the Thames

Little Toot Through the Golden Gate

The Littles, by John Peterson. New York: Scholastic, 1970.

The Littles and the Big Storm

The Littles and Their Friends

The Littles and the Trash Tinnier

The Littles Have a Wedding

The Littles' Surprise Party

The Littles to the Rescue

Tom Little's Great Halloween Scare

Madeline, by Ludwig Bemelmans. New York: Viking Press, 1939.

Madeline and the Bad Hat

Madeline and the Gypsies

Madeline in London

Madeline's Rescue

The Moffats, by Eleanor Estes. Illustrated by Louis Slobodkin. New York: Harcourt Brace Jovanovich, 1968.

Rufus M.

The Middle Moffat

The Magician's Nephew, by C. S. Lewis. New York: Macmillan Publishing Co., 1970.

The Lion, the Witch, and the Wardrobe, 1951

The Horse and His Boy, 1954

Prince Caspian, 1951

The Voyage of the Dawn Treader, 1952

The Silver Chair, 1953

The Last Battle, 1956

Ramona the Pest, by Beverly Cleary. Illustrated by Louis Darling. New York: Dell Publishing Co., 1982.

Ramona and Her Father

Ramona and Her Mother

Ramona and Her Friends

Ramona Quimby, Age 8

Ramona the Brave

A Stranger at Greene Knowe, by Lucy Boston. Illustrated by Peter Boston. New York: Harcourt Brace Jovanovich, 1979.

(Green Knowe is the setting for other novels by Lucy Boston.)

The Wonderful Flight to the Mushroom Planet by Eleanor Cameron. Illustrated by Robert Henneberger. Boston: Little, Brown and Co., 1954.

(There are five additional Mushroom Planet books.)

The Wonderful Story of Henry Sugar and Six More. by Roald Dahl. New York: Knopf, 1977. Bantam, 1979.

HEROES *AND* HEROINES *AND* THRILLS:
BOOKS *FOR* AGES SIX *TO* TWELVE *TO* LISTEN *TO AND* READ

Guidelines for Choosing Adventure Stories

1. Bear your child's interests, likes, and dislikes in mind, and choose an adventure that fits.
2. Choose adventures for reading aloud that are considerably more advanced than his or her independent reading level.
3. Choose adventures that are inventive but have an atmosphere of reality.
4. Choose stories with spirited plots.

The Adventures of Tom Sawyer, by Mark Twain. New York: Airmont Publishing Co., 1964.

The Black Stallion, by Walter Farley. New York: Random House, 1977.

Caddie Woodlawn, by Carol Brink. New York: Macmillan Publishing Co., 1973.

Call It Courage, by Armstrong Sperry. New York: Macmillan Publishing Co., 1971.

Captain Grey, by Avi. New York: Pantheon Books, 1977.

The Case of the Baker Street Irregular, by Robert Newman. New York: Atheneum Publishing Co., 1978.

The Case of the Snowbound Spy, by Edmund Hildick. New York: Macmillan Publishing Co., 1980.

The Courage of Sarah Noble, by Alice Dalgliesh. New York: Charles Scribner's Sons, 1954.

The Door in the Wall, by Marguerite De Angeli. New York: Doubleday, 1949.

Escape from Warsaw, by Ian Serraillier. New York: Scholastic, 1972.

The Half-a-Moon Inn, by Paul Fleischman. New York: Harper and Row, 1979.

Hans Brinker; or The Silver Skates, by Mary Mapes Dodge. New York: Putnam Publishing Group, 1963.

Harriet, the Spy, by Louise Fitzhugh. New York: Harper and Row, 1964.

The Hobbit; or, There and Back Again, by J. R. R. Tolkien. Boston: Houghton Mifflin Co., 1966.

The House with a Clock in Its Walls, by John Bellairs. New York: Dial Press, 1973.

The Incredible Journey, by Sheila Burnford. New York: Bantam Books, 1981.

Ironhead, by Mel Ellis. New York: Archway Paperbacks, 1970.

The Island of the Blue Dolphins, by Scott O'Dell. New York: Dell Publishing Co., 1982.

Jumanji, by Chris Van Allsburg. Boston: Houghton Mifflin Co., 1981.

The Mouse and His Child, by Russell Hoban. New York: Avon Books, 1982.

My Brother, the Wind, by G. Clifton Wisler. New York: Doubleday, 1979.

Oliver Twist, by Charles Dickens. New York: Bantam Books, 1981.

Otto of the Silver Hand, by Howard Pyle. New York: Charles Scribner's Sons, 1954.

Over Sea, over Stone, by Susan Cooper. New York: Harcourt Brace Jovanovich, 1979.

The Princess and the Lion, by Elizabeth Coatsworth. New York: Pantheon Books, 1963.

Robinson Crusoe, by Daniel Defoe. New York: Charles Scribner's Sons, 1958.

Sarah Bishop, by Scott O'Dell. Boston: Houghton Mifflin Co., 1980.

The Secret of the Andes, by Ann Nolan Clark. New York: Viking Press, 1952.

Susannah and the Blue House Mystery, by Patricia Elmore. New York: E. P. Dutton, 1979.

The Sword and the Grail, retold by Constance Hieatt. New York: Thomas Y. Crowell Co., 1972.

The Three Musketeers, by Alexandre Dumas. New York: Putnam Publishing Group, 1982.

Tintin in Tibet, by Herge. Boston: Little, Brown and Co., 1975.

Toliver's Secret, by Esther Wood Brady. New York: Crown Publishers, 1976.

Treasure Island, by Robert Louis Stevenson. New York: Putnam Publishing Group, 1981.

The Winter When Time Was Frozen, by Els Pelgrom. New York: William Morrow and Co., 1980.

The Wish at the Top, by Clyde Robert Bulla. New York: Thomas Y. Crowell Co., 1974.

The Wolves of Willoughby Chase, by Joan Aiken. New York: Dell Publishing Co., 1981.

COOKBOOKS *for* AGES SIX *to* TWELVE

Betty Crocker's Cookbook for Boys and Girls. New York: Western Publishing Co., 1975.

The Fairy Tale Cookbook, by Carol MacGregor. New York: Macmillan Publishing Co., 1972.

The Pooh Cookbook, by Virginia Ellison. New York: Dell Publishing Co., 1975.

Science Experiments You Can Eat, by Vicki Cobb. New York: Harper and Row, 1972.

The Wind in the Willows Country Cookbook, by Arabella Boxer. New York: Charles Scribner's Sons, 1983.

The titles of additional books with carefully selected recommended reading lists may be found in the Appendix.

BOOK CLUBS FOR CHILDREN AGES SIX TO TWELVE

Hardcover

Grow-with-Me Book Club, Garden City, NY 11530 ($2.49 per book)

   Growing Readers' Books

Junior Literary Guild, Garden City, NY, 11530 ($2.95 per book)

   Easy Reading (ages 7 and 8)

   Intermediate (ages 9 to 11)

I Can Read Book Club, 1250 Fairwood Ave., Columbus, OH 43216 ($1.89 per book) (ages 4 to 8)

Parents' Magazine Read Aloud and Easy Reading Program, Box 161, Bergenfield, NJ 07621 ($1.95 per book) (ages 4 to 8)

Weekly Reader Children's Book Club, 1250 Fairwood Ave., Columbus, OH 43216 ($1.89 per book) (ages 5 to 7, 8 to 9, 10 to 11)

School Book Clubs (Paperback)

Firefly Book Club, Reader's Digest Services, Pleasantville, NY 10570 (average of $.50 per book) (second and third grades)

Scholastic Book Clubs, 904 Sylvan Ave., Englewood Cliffs, NJ 07632 ($.30–$.50 per book)

   See-Saw Book Program (kindergarten and first grade)

   Lucky Book Club (second and third grades)

   Arrow Book Club (fourth to sixth grades)

Young Readers Press, Simon and Schuster, 1 West 39th St., NY 10018 ($.40–$.95 per book)

   King Cole Book Club (kindergarten and first grade)

   Willie Whale Book Club (second and third grades)

   Falcon Book Club (fourth to sixth grades)

Xerox Paperback Book Club, Box 1195, Education Center, Columbus, OH 43216 ($.30–$.70 per book)

   Buddy Books (kindergarten and first grade)

   Goodtime Books (second and third grades)

Discovering Books (fourth to sixth grades)

For more complete information on children's book clubs, see Nancy Larrick's *A Parent's Guide to Children's Reading* (Philadelphia: Westminster Press, 1982).

MAGAZINES FOR AGES SIX TO TWELVE

Boy's Life, 1325 Walnut Hill Lane, Irving, TX, 75062.

Children's Digest, 1100 Waterway Blvd., Box 567, Indianapolis, IN, 46206.

Cobblestones, 20 Grove Street, Peterboro, NH, 03458.

Cricket, 1058 Eighth Street, Box 100, La Salle, IL, 61301.

The Electric Company Magazine, One Lincoln Plaza, New York, NY, 10023.

Highlights, 2300 W. 5th Avenue, Box 269, Columbus, OH, 43272-0002.

Jack and Jill, 1100 Waterway Blvd., Box 567, Indianapolis, IL, 46206.

Nautica, Pickering Wharf, Salem, MA, 01970.

Odyssey, 625 E. St. Paul Avenue, Box 92788, Milwaukee, WI, 53202.

Popular Science, 380 Madison Avenue, New York, NY, 10017.

Ranger Rick's Nature Magazine, National Wildlife Federation, 1412 16th St., N. W., Washington D. C., 20036.

Sesame Street Magazine, One Lincoln Plaza, New York, NY, 10023.

Stone Soup: A Magazine by Children, Box 83, Santa Cruz, CA, 95063.

3-2-1 Contact, One Lincoln Plaza, New York, NY, 10023.

PART THREE

AGES TWELVE THROUGH SIXTEEN: Bridging the Gap Between Childhood and Adult Reading

CHAPTER EIGHT

Keeping Reading Alive

> All good books are alike in that they are truer than if they had really happened, and after you are finished reading one you will feel that all that happened to you, and afterwards it all belongs to you: the good and the bad, the ecstasy, the remorse and sorrow, the people and the places and how the weather was.
>
> —Ernest Hemingway, "Old Newsman Writes"

MANY OF YOU, AS YOU COME TO THIS SECTION, are apt to be parents who are already distressed over their youngster's lack of reading prowess or lack of interest in reading. You can't go back and take your child through the baby steps of reading, but you can still excite your child about reading at whatever developmental stage he has now attained.

Whether your child is a reader or a youngster who only reads when he has to, your goal is the same, to ensure that your child continues to grow as a reader. In this phase of your child's reading development, there are two things that need to be done to stimulate that growth. First, you need to guide your youngster to the kinds of personally relevant reading that will reinforce a commitment to print as a means of experiencing and knowing. Second, you need to help him meet the challenges posed by increasingly more complex and abstract writing.

You can accomplish both ends by doing exactly what

parents do when their children are tiny infants—help them to experience literary language in a personal way. Even though your child is either verging on adolescence or is already there, the procedure is virtually the same one described in chapter 2. First, you make sure your child has contact with literature, and next, you help him do things that will stimulate emotional and intellectual responses. Then, just as before, you repeat the process whenever the opportunity presents itself.

You're now moving into a period of time when influencing your child to read and write—which he must do if he is to continue to grow as a reader—is going to take greater subtlety and will often be less effective. You can push, but as they become teenagers, youngsters don't always move in the direction of your push. In fact, they tend to push back. If you wish to have the same effect as you had when your word and your approval and your suggestions were central to your child's feelings of worth and self-esteem you have to interact with him in ways he can accept. This needn't be a particularly difficult time with your child, but there will be times when "Oh, Mommy" or "Oh, Daddy" will signal your child's defense of his independence.

Children at this age are in the business of creating independent personas, and that makes it more difficult to effect changes in the courses they may have set for themselves. Things won't always happen between you and your teenager on an "I tell you what to do, and this is what you do" basis. To help your child now, you have to be even more sensitive to his states of mind and interests and must redouble your efforts to personalize his reading program.

The specific goals and suggestions that follow are intended to help you guide your child to a deeper understanding and appreciation of both fiction and nonfiction reading. This deepening is really the difference between reading and being "a reader." More basically, though, they are intended to help you to help your child discover, either for the first time or anew, that reading enriches life.

Goal 1: Developing Personal Responses to Literature

The adolescent years and the period just preceding adolescence are marked by constant seeking of personal and social definition. It seems almost as if youngsters in this phase of life are continually holding themselves up for inspection—looking inward to measure their growth, their feelings, their thinking. At the same time they are looking outward for solutions to personal problems, for outlets for fears and impulses, for feelings of mastery, for opportunities to try on different identities. While books can be a powerful resource for any child, they are particularly so for an adolescent. In the words of Bruno Bettelheim, Professor Emeritus of Education, Child Psychology, and Psychoanalysis at the University of Chicago, stories can help to clarify emotions, give realization to anxieties and aspirations, and suggest solutions to problems. All too often this resource is ignored.

Literature is my Utopia. Here I am not disfranchised. No barrier of the senses shuts me out from the sweet, gracious discourse of my book friends. They talk to me without embarrassment or awkwardness.
—*Helen Keller,* The Story of My Life

Even if your youngster has been a reader up to this point, if he follows the typical pattern, books may seem less compelling now that he is an adolescent or is soon to become one. His preference in this phase of life may well be for direct or more immediate experience. Sports, spectator events, parties, shopping, the media, or being with friends will all take precedence over reading, unless he discovers reading matter that satisfies some of his deep-felt needs. This is where your youngster needs your help now—help in finding those things to read.

When a young person has a piece of written material in his hands that relates to his true interests, causes him to identify with a character or a situation, or speaks to unexpressed desires or fears, the effect is remarkable. No matter if the youngster is an eager or a reluctant reader, when the material is personally important, that youngster wants to read. Jerry, one of my students at UCLA's Fernald School and not a strong reader, was interested in birds of prey. It was a deep interest of his, not a passing fancy. We went to great lengths to find material for Jerry about birds of prey, but we found that virtually nothing in depth about the subject had been written at the fourth-grade level, at which he was then reading. For lack of an alternative, I brought Jerry an article from the *National Geographic.* He read every word.

Records indicate that young people read almost completely for experience. They want to experience adventure and excitement or to feel tenderness and caring, to enjoy imaginative wandering, to know the feeling of self-sufficiency without adult domination, to experience life in various historical periods and cultural patterns, to feel the frustration and despair of the psychological deviate. Reading makes possible the living of a thousand lives instead of one.
    —G. Robert Carlsen, Books and the Teenage Reader: A
        Guide for Teachers, Libraries, and Parents

To keep your youngster developing as a lifelong reader, you must keep him reading. You can do much to achieve this goal by mounting a home reading program built around reading matter that can contribute in the specific and personal ways outlined above to your youngster's search for personal directions. It matters little what the material is; if it's relevant to your young reader's concerns, he will have a rewarding personal experience and will continue to read.

Your child will, no doubt, be reading things that you are going to feel uncomfortable with. Many adolescents and preadolescents go through a phase when all they choose to read are junk magazines and books—lurid comics, gossip and scandal journals, and pulp romances. Both the subjects of this material and the gutsy language they use appeal to a youngster's desire to experience the world. Unless the phase persists, it does little harm. In fact, this kind of written material can actually improve a poor reader's skills, because it motivates him to read.

SUGGESTION: Use your youngster's own reading choices as clues to his interests.

You may prohibit your child, as some parents do, from reading certain kinds of books and magazines in the home, but your youngster will still have easy access to whatever he wants to read. If the desire is strong enough, he will probably continue to read the forbidden material despite your protestation. If he does follow your dictates, he may lose his only source of reading pleasure. Neither of these outcomes contributes to your child's progress in becoming a lifelong reader.

I try never to criticize anything a child is reading. A little of "junk" is okay—as long as you introduce other things.
—Ami Kirby, Director of Children's Services, Santa Monica Public Library, Santa Monica, California

---

Rather than censor or criticize, talk to your child about the kinds of things he looks for in his reading. Ask him to tell you about some of the stories he is reading and note what kinds of things excite him. When you know what vicarious thrills he finds in junk reading, you know what to look for when you go to the library or the bookstore for a good book that he will enjoy—which is exactly what you will do next. With this kind of positive intervention, you won't have a resentful teenager on your hands, you will have, instead, a teenager who is reading something he wants to read.

SUGGESTION: Help your child discover young adult literature.

For reading to be sufficiently compelling to compete with more direct sources of experience, it must be something that is close to your youngster's own experience and provides some answers to personal dilemmas. At this age level, there still seems to be a fairly stereotypic breakdown of boys' and girls' concerns. Girls tend to be more interested in interpersonal relationships and the development of intimacy. Boys, on the other hand, appear to be more concerned with the formation of personal identity. Nevertheless, for both boys and girls, the story that offers a hero or a heroine with whom the reader can identify and also provides a solution to personal problems is the kind of reading material that will keep them reading.

> *For a story truly to hold the child's attention, it must entertain him and arouse his curiosity. But to enrich his life, it must stimulate his imagination; help him to develop his intellect and to clarify his emotions; be attuned to his anxieties and aspirations; give full recognition to his difficulties, while at the same time suggesting solutions to the problems which perturb him. In short, it must at one and the same time relate to all aspects of his personality—and this without ever belittling but, on the contrary, giving full credence to the seriousness of the child's predicaments, while simultaneously promoting confidence in himself and in his future.*
> —*Bruno Bettelheim*, The Uses of Enchantment

For today's teen and preteen readers, there is a wealth of material available that did not exist fifteen or twenty years ago. This greatly simplifies your job of finding compelling and appropriate reading matter for your youngster. The young adult category of publishing has become one of the largest and most profitable of divisions for mass-market publishers. The most effective way to personalize your youngster's reading program is to go to a bookstore and ask for the addresses of various publishers that put out young adult fiction and nonfiction. Then simply write to the sales departments requesting full catalogs. You will get back list

after list after list of books. You can give these to your youngster to help him select books that he might not know about,
or you can use the lists yourself to help you locate just the
perfect book to give to your child.

---

*Teenagers read adult books from every genre. . . . Much of
their dramatic reading comes from the adult reservoir. . . .
Teen readers [also] have an enthusiasm for accounts of personal experience which borders on the bizarre or unusual,
such as being stranded in the Andes by a plane wreck* (Alive)
or living among wolves (Never Cry Wolf). *In general, fiction
is the principal form of adult literature that adolescents read,
and they are highly selective in their choice.*
　　—G. Robert Carlsen, Books and the Teenage Reader: A
　　　　　　Guide for Teachers, Libraries, and Parents

It may seem like a bother to go through publishers' lists,
but if you want the "right" book—the one that will fit your
youngster's special interests and needs—this effort is one
that pays off. Most published material is not available on the
racks of any one bookstore or in any one community. Your
particular town may have no large interest in books of mountain adventures for young readers. If you have a child who
is interested in mountain adventure, he is out of luck. But
with publishers' lists you have access to a world of material
that may never show up in your local bookshops. Your child
may find a whole series of mountain adventures in the publishers' catalogs. Then it will just be a matter of ordering the
books your child wants from the bookstore, who will get
them from the publisher. Or he can order directly from the
publisher—all publishers include ordering information along
with their lists.

If you prefer you can simply go to your local bookstore
and say, "Can I look through your catalogs of books available from publishers?" You can then look at them and order
directly in that way.

The books that will do the most to maintain your youngster's interest in reading during early adolescence and, at the

same time, help to bridge the gap between children's and adult literature are the young adult novels. Because these books are usually close to youngsters' own experience, they tend to elicit a high degree of personal response. Among the vast literature for this age group are two new genres for you to consider for your youngster's home reading program.

One of the most popular genres of reading material among this age group in recent years consists of teen romantic fiction for girls. These romances are generally about a fifteen- to sixteen-year-old, most often a girl, and are told from that character's point of view. Typically the plots have to do with falling in love for the first time. In the course of the action, the problems these new emotions and social interactions provoke are explored. Examination of such feelings as insecurity, uncertainty, unpopularity, inferiority, pleasure and pain, struggles for independence—all of which problems are particularly acute for this age group—make these books relevant to young teen and preteen readers. And since, as in fairy tales, the romantic conflicts inevitably result in the hero or heroine's growth, increased confidence, and happiness, they leave the young reader with feelings of optimism, a fact that makes these romances even more appealing.

You will find a wellspring of reading material that speaks to girls' concerns in these teen romances. Perhaps a thousand titles are currently available, and at least ten new ones appear each month. Your youngster can order two new Wildfire Romances each month through Scholastic Book Services' Teenage Book Club for as little as ninety-five cents per book. For a listing of teen romance series refer to the Suggested Reading section at the end of Part Three.

Even if your youngster seems at first to be an incurable addict of these unrealistic formula romances, try not to be unduly concerned. Though their literary quality sometimes leaves much to be desired, teen romances provide both enjoyment and understanding of self and others—both primary goals in any reading program.

> *Records show that most teens are hooked on the reading experience through juvenile series books, which are thus a normal stage in one's reading growth.*
> —G. Robert Carlsen, Books and the Teenage Reader: A
> Guide for Teachers, Libraries, and Parents

And you needn't worry. Your young reader will eventually tire of the formula and will be receptive to more mature treatment of male-female relationships. When that time comes you will want to promote your youngster to historical romances, fiction that will still capture her romantic imagination but at the same time give her the experience of reading quality literature.

> *Most adolescent novels are pop novels. They are honestly written and fairly accurate in their recording of human experience. They are often exciting reading but they lack enduring qualities. They often deal with a momentary problem of the teen scene. At the moment subjects with high appeal are alcoholism, child abuse, homosexuality and rape."*
> —G. Robert Carlsen, Books and the Teenage Reader: A
> Guide for Teachers, Librarians, and Parents

Another form of teen fiction that is extremely popular with both boys and girls is the adolescent problem novel. These books, unlike the frothy teen romances, treat contemporary social questions in a frank and realistic way. Instead of first love, these books treat of the first love affair, abortion, drug abuse, alcoholism, or other problems that many teenagers in today's society confront. You may well object to some of the attitudes and ideas expressed in these books, but these are books your young reader will want to read, because they teach him about the world as experienced by other teenagers. And they give him ideas for handling his own problems. For that reason, if for no other, you may want to suggest them to your youngster to read. For a listing of young adult problem novels refer to the Suggested Reading section at the end of Part Three.

One of the driving forces in a twelve- to seventeen-year-old's life is the search for a hero to emulate in his own life. A home reading program that will keep a teenager reading is a program that recognizes the teenager's need to try on different hats in his search for a niche in the world.

SUGGESTION: Select books for your youngster's home reading program that have strong characters with whom he can identify.

Any book in which the hero or heroine wins acclaim for some quality of mind, body, or character that makes him or her stand out among ordinary folk is a book that will claim teenagers' attention. But to be sure the book is right for your youngster, there is one more factor to consider: The character should either be involved in an activity your youngster is interested in or should be tackling a problem similar to one your youngster is wrestling with. If your child is already a reader, he will lose himself to this kind of book experience. If he is having trouble warming to reading, he will respond to a book that fits in with a need or desire of his.

SUGGESTION: Supply books to read that will provide outlets for fears and impulses.

You will have no trouble finding the books you want. They range from novels like Charles Dickens's *A Tale of Two Cities* to Ralph Ellison's *The Invisible Man* to biographies of contemporary sports figures, such as Mary Louise Rettor and Kareem Abdul-Jabbar. Your only problem will be to narrow down the choices to those that are relevant to your youngster's concerns and interests. For a listing of books that contain heroes, heroines, and thrills for young adults refer to the Suggested Reading section at the end of Part Three.

Most libraries keep their own up-to-date lists of books that make "good reading" for junior high school students. For more complete lists in which books are classified according to subject matter, ask your librarian for the *Junior High School Library Catalog.* Both will aid you in your search for good books that speak to teenagers' needs and desires.

Students who do not read or who read non-fiction exclusively deprive themselves of those literary materials that seem critical to the education of the imagination and to higher-order skills of reading. Thus it is not surprising that their performance is lower than those who read fiction or poetry or both fiction and non-fiction.

—Reading Comprehension of American Youth, *National Assessment of Educational Progress, Education Commission of the States*

The years from twelve to seventeen are a time when youngsters dream of adventures that will test their courage and confirm their value to themselves and others. These years are also a time when fears of failure, rejection, scorn —even of death—lie just beneath the surface of the emotions. For the majority of teenagers, the only possible outlet for these impulses and fears is in the vicarious experience offered through the media or through reading.

You can further enhance your reading program's appeal by including adventure stories peopled with courageous characters who overcome all obstacles to accomplish their goals—and in the process leave your youngster breathless with apprehension. In addition to historical and contemporary accounts of the conquests and adventures of real people, such as Anne Frank's *The Diary of a Young Girl* or Thor Heyerdahl's *The Voyage of the Ra,* you will want to stock your youngster's reading shelf with fictional tales of daring. Identification with these real-life and fictional heroes and heroines will help your youngster find an outlet through imagination for his own impulses and fears.

Goal 2: Responding to Reading Through Writing

Few teenagers are content to just read and leave it at that. If an adventure thrills, they want to share their reactions to those thrills with friends. Listen in on a teen conversation about a book one of them has read, and you will be treated to a blow-by-blow recital of the dramatic action. Unlike the retellings offered by younger children, the teenager's account will be interspersed with personal reactions to characters and plot. In the telling the speaker redefines the adventure in terms of his own personal response. As a result, the original experience takes on added meaning.

If the redefinition of a literary experience comes in the form of writing, the experience becomes even more personal and more meaningful. Therefore, the surest way to deepen an adolescent's sense of personal engagement and develop his or her responses to both fiction and nonfiction is to encourage him to write.

The following suggestions will give you some ideas for writing projects that will satisfy your adolescent's need to share and to act upon literary ideas that he finds personally relevant.

SUGGESTION: Engage your youngster in issue-oriented writing projects.

Whatever else it is, adolescence is a time for commitment. Just as youngsters hold themselves up for scrutiny, they also hold society up for critical appraisal. When they find society wanting in areas they care about, they rush to the remedy. Teachers of this age group know they have only to introduce an emotional subject like the annual slaughter of baby seals to start animal lovers on vigorous letter-writing campaigns.

Your reading program can profit from your youngster's inclination to take positions and to broadcast feelings. Just add a writing adjunct. One way to get your youngster started on writing is to provide him with reading material that raises questions of justice, humanity, or fairness in relation to a subject that interests him. You will almost certainly be guaranteed a reaction.

To channel your youngster's response into writing, suggest that he write letters of protest to newspaper editors, politicians, and public interest organizations, or suggest he write a short story or poem about what is bothering him. A third possibility is to suggest that he develop a specific plan for tackling the problem.

Books that focus on cultural diversity, expressive needs, freedom of choice for all people can encourage children to explore, question and actively participate in their society.
—Characters in Textbooks, *a review of the literature,
United States Commission on Civil Rights*

Prominent among teenage causes are preservation of the environment, fair treatment of minorities, cessation of cruelty to animals, and prevention of nuclear holocaust. Yet these are only a small fraction of the societal problems that teenagers get steamed up about. Your youngster may have quite a different set of concerns. You can tap into these by being alert to any reading matter that relates to your teenager's particular interests. Newspaper and magazine articles and appeals are the most readily available source of issue-oriented reading matter. And both fiction and nonfiction books that treat of general existential problems, as well as specific contemporary problems, abound in adolescent literature.

To find these things, you might use the *Reader's Guide to Periodical Literature.* Or look up subject guides to *Books in Print.* Look for a title that would appeal to your child. Both of these references are available in public libraries.

And if your youngster is particularly keen on a subject, you might want to invest in some books as gifts. For a listing of issue-oriented books refer to the Suggested Reading section at the end of Part Three.

The writing projects that follow reading may take many forms. The simplest forms of response are the letters of protest or support. At this age your youngster won't need much help in getting a letter-writing project going. But you can still show your interest by considering along with him the appropriate recipient for these letters. Many adolescents have little knowledge about who can make things happen in our society, and your suggestions will be welcome. If you can't provide the answers, suggest that your youngster call the reference desk at the public library for information.

Your youngster's response may also take the form of a personal solution to the problem. Following his reading of a book that points up the inhumane treatment of animals in animal shelters, you might suggest that instead of just lamenting the plight of animals, he develop a written plan for a new type of animal-care institution. In order to prepare his plan, he can perhaps get additional information from a local animal group. There are hundreds of national organizations that always appreciate interest in their cause and need help. Once again, your youngster's best source of information on organizations is the reference librarian.

If your child shows any inclination to write, you would do well to give him a blank book in which to jot down ideas and notes on the subject he is exploring, or in which to write poems and stories. There are beautiful blank books available for all ages. They are decorated with everything from teddy bears to pinups, from animals to zodiac signs. Sometimes just having a blank book around will serve as an inspiration for putting thoughts about self, others, and the world into writing. And of course, one of the things that you as a parent must do is let your child know you respect the privacy of the communication.

If your youngster is unsure of his ideas or how to develop them in writing for public consumption, you can greatly ease the process by making yourself available for a writing conference, just as you did when your child was younger.

The first thing to do is to suggest that you talk about some of the things your youngster might want to put into a letter, a proposal, or a story. Then suggest that he jot down a word or two for each of the ideas he explores. All he needs to complete a plan of attack is to number his ideas according to some logical order. This quick, rough outline will give him the confidence he needs to proceed.

Once your youngster has a plan of attack, your role in the project is simply to stop and listen when he has something to share.

Writing in general often requires other people to stimulate discussion, to provide spellings, to listen to choice phrases, and even just for companionship in an activity that can be so personal and unpredictable that it creates considerable stress. Especially when writing is being learned, there is often a great need for and advantage in people working together on a letter, poem, or story.

Frank Smith, Essays into Literacy

Despite adolescents' need to assert their autonomy, they still look to their parents for encouragement and advice. By stopping and listening when your youngster had something to share, by knowing your youngster's concerns and needs, and by suggesting literary avenues for learning and experiencing, you have kept your youngster's interest in reading high.

Now it's time to do what you have been aiming for since your child was a tiny infant—take your child into the vast world of literature that addresses the more mature mind and psyche.

CHAPTER NINE

Making the Transition to Adult Reading

> 'Tis the good reader that makes the good book; in
> every book he finds passages which seem confidences
> or asides hidden from all else and unmistakably meant
> for his ear; the profit of books is according to the sensi-
> bility of the reader; the profoundest thought or passion
> sleeps as in a mine, until it is discovered by an equal
> mind and heart.
> —Ralph Waldo Emerson, *Society and Solitude*

AS A TEACHER, I have always been convinced that children
are far more intellectually capable than we ever give them
credit for and that they need only a little stimulation to prove
what they can do. But I never really put my belief to the test
until forced to do so by governmental regulations.

It happened in France, toward the end of the sixties. I
had taken a job as an English teacher at the Ecole Active
Bilingue in Paris. As I was to discover, however, I was expected to teach without books. The tight foreign exchange
regulations of that period had made it impossible for either
the school or commercial bookstores to purchase foreign
textbooks.

I was desperate. I had scores of English, American, and

French children between the ages of ten and fourteen waiting for me to teach them English, and I had no books. The only thing I could think to do was read aloud to them, and the only material I had that seemed at all appropriate was a collection of English and American short stories. So that's what I read, and that's what we discussed.

I quickly discovered there is nothing like exposure to adult literature to engage children's minds. The children, even the youngest, listened—and then talked about what they heard—at a level of interest and insight that I had never before been able to stimulate in a classroom.

These were not especially talented children. In fact, because of their parents' nomadic life-styles, a majority of them came to me with serious academic problems. They were simply children who were excited by the opportunity to think and talk about the ways of the world from an adult perspective.

In this final step of your make-your-child-a-lifelong-reader program you will learn how you can give your child the opportunity to extend both her literary horizons and the ability to interpret what she reads.

Goal: Promoting Your Youngster's Intellectual Responses to Complex Literary Forms

The years between ages eleven and seventeen are years when children's intellectual growth enables them to gain insight into new aspects of literary content and structure. During this period they not only can but—if the opportunity arises—*will* begin to become adept at going beyond the explicit information offered by the author.

The ability to extend interpretation of text beyond the literal develops at a very young age. In chapters 3 and 4 you learned how you could develop your young child's physical, emotional, and intellectual responses to simple literature, but not until she reaches a more mature stage of cognitive development is a reader able to bring to the text a sufficient knowledge of relations between people and of situations to be able to fill in the gaps an author will typically leave in literary works.

A practiced reader at this stage of development doesn't have to be told by the author that young Manola, the matador's son in *Shadow of a Bull,* a young adult novel by Maia Wojciechowska, fears bulls and is shaken by his realization of his cowardice and the shame it will bring upon the family. The more mature reader responds to the cues the author gives to infer Manola's thoughts, intentions, and feelings. Only by being able to make such inferences can a reader fully comprehend as well as appreciate what an author is trying to say.

Because the meaning of text is only partially determined by the text itself, reading must be an inferential, constructive process, characterized by the formation and testing of hypotheses or models about what the text is "about," a process similar in many ways to problem solving.
—Rand J. Spiro et al., Theoretical Issues in Reading
Comprehension

In addition to their developing perception of character, readers in this age group are capable of producing and interpreting metaphors and discovering social truths in humor and satire. To make your child a lifelong reader, you need to tap into this newfound capacity for interpretive response to literature. You do this just as you have done before: Make sure your youngster has a broad range of literary experience that includes listening, reading, seeing, talking, and writing. The following suggestions will help you stimulate your youngster's literary growth and keep her reading.

You can give your child the opportunity to extend both her literary horizons and her ability to interpret what she reads by organizing reading and discussion sessions that include the whole family and by making them a regular family event.

SUGGESTION: **Provide opportunities for your youngster to listen to adult literature.**

For a successful family read-aloud session, you need to do a little advance planning. First you need to decide upon a time and a place. You need to choose a time when all the members of your family are likely to be available and at ease, but the formalities should end there. Your reading get-together could be an after dinner event one night a week when the family eats together. It doesn't matter where or when it occurs, just as long as the individual family members feel good about being there.

Then you need to choose the reading material. I suggest that you start with short stories. They are ideal because an entire story can be read in one session. But more important, they are a compelling literary form, one not only rich in language but structured to provide emotional and intellectual impact. The choice of subject matter is something you must decide for yourself. Here, you need to use your knowledge of your own family members—their ages, their interests, their biases. If you encounter any difficulty in finding something from contemporary literature that will suit everybody, look for a folktale, a legend, or a myth. These traditional forms will provide all the literary and intellectual depth that you could ever want, yet will captivate all the members of your family. For a listing of stories for family reading sessions refer to the Suggested Reading section at the end of Part Three.

The reader should be the member of the family with the most dramatic reading ability. Unless your youngster is already a skillful reader, don't ask her to fill this role. This is not a time to practice reading skills; this is a time for her to grow in understanding and appreciation of mature literature. You may want to vary the program from time to time by sharing the responsibility for reading. Choose a narrator to read the narrational parts and parcel out the character roles among the other members of the family. Each person will then read the speeches of "his" or "her" character. This is an effective way to develop personal responses to and interpretation of character traits. Do this only occasionally, however —and then only if a child is a secure reader.

Now that you're ready to proceed, all you and your family have to do is listen, enjoy, and then share the things that moved you and the ideas that attracted you.

SUGGESTION: Use the media to help your youngster experience literature.

The 1982 National Assessment of Educational Progress revealed that most teenagers read on their own for less than one hour a day. By contrast, one-half of the thirteen-year-olds and one-third of the seventeen-year-olds surveyed watched television three hours or more a day. Although no statistics are available on the amount of time adolescents and preadolescents spend listening to music, that activity is thought to be even more popular than TV viewing.

What makes these media so compelling is their ability to help youngsters to experience and feel immediately. Visual media (TV, movies, video) and aural media (records, cassettes, radio) have a decided advantage over print media: they have the capability of transmitting experience directly. They can also reach the emotions directly. Since they are so powerful, you need to make the media work for you in your reading program.

When you combine media and literature, you both heighten the adolescent's literary experience and stimulate her interpretive thinking. Recordings, films, and radio dramatizations can all familiarize your child with gradually more intellectually challenging literary works, works that, by their nature encourage intellectual responses.

With all media activities, the inherent educational value can only be fully realized if your youngster talks about the experience. In learning to respond to media presentations, no matter what form they take, youngsters learn to use language to discover, examine, and create meaning. And of course these skills are directly applicable to the discovery of meaning in literature.

Your first ally is the media form that is most closely related to reading—the tape recording of a book. Recordings of books provide a means of extending your family reading sessions into longer works, such as novels and plays. And because the readers are dramatic artists, the grandeur of literature and the emotional effect of the experience will provide an added dimension to your family program.

In choosing books on tapes that encourage interpretation, try to find works with unfamiliar themes, themes that will awaken your youngster to new areas of experience and thought. Science fiction will fill that bill admirably, but you'll want to get into other genres of literature, too. Mystery, fantasy, adventure, and romance are all available on tape. Bookstores, libraries, and book tape rental agencies all have them.

In addition to your regular home readings, you might consider taking tapes along with you on holidays or weekend trips. You will find the time spent in getting to your destination much more pleasurable if you have an exciting adventure or a historical account of the area to listen to along the route.

After you and your child have listened to and talked about the reading, suggest that your youngster borrow the book from the library to read independently. The knowledge of the book that she gained from hearing it on tape will greatly ease any difficulties your youngster might have with reading.

Watching movies and dramatizations of literature on television can also help your child to develop further insights into characters' motives, feelings, intentions, and thoughts— providing you couple that viewing with talk about the film. A TV series like "Star Trek," while perhaps not what we normally think of as literature, is nonetheless high-quality science fiction. Watching it can give youngsters a sense of the dramatic structure of that genre, as well as provide insights into interpersonal relationships.

When this kind of written-to-formula production becomes so familiar that your youngster ceases to think while viewing, you can increase her intellectual involvement by making a family game of turning off the sound and filling in the dialogue yourselves. Or you can get your child to summarize story lines by asking, "Did you see 'Star Trek' last night? What happened?"

If the drama your youngster plans to watch promises to be challenging because of its theme or the issues it tackles —such as "The Day After," the story of a town devastated by nuclear missiles—you can make the experience more meaningful by talking about the content in advance. Prior knowledge will help your youngster interpret more fully the events leading up to and following the holocaust, and the characters' actions, thoughts, and feelings in the aftermath of the destruction. A brief and casual conversation is all that is necessary to alert your child to the underlying themes in the film. Then after you've watched the production together, share your reactions.

SUGGESTION: Couple listening and viewing sessions with discussion.

The value of the discussion that follows a story or a film lies in its power to illuminate and clarify your youngster's emotional and intellectual responses to the literary work. When you start a conversation following the family reading or viewing activity, bear in mind that you simply want to help your child develop greater awareness of her own experience. You can accomplish this aim by focusing on the reaction of the listener to the work she heard.

When you initiate a discussion, you will want to channel it so your family talks first about the world of the story as if that world were not, in fact, fictional. Get as many family members as possible to talk about their reactions to key episodes and characters and to express their likes and dislikes for them. Encourage them to conjecture about what might have happened to the characters in the "past" or what might happen to them in the "future." Or encourage them to relate the fictional incidents depicted to similar things that they themselves have experienced in real life.

A story that is highly charged with emotion, such as Shirley Jackson's "The Lottery," stimulates its own discussion. Your youngster will be anxious to share her feelings about the unexpected stoning of the lottery winner and the dispassionate way the townspeople follow the lottery process. A simple question like "Well, what did you think?" can unleash a flood of reaction. Once the family members begin to share their reactions, they will spontaneously begin to talk about what they thought something meant or about elements they didn't quite understand.

Your role is to act as moderator and participant in these discussions and to ask questions that will cause family members to explain a personal response or defend an interpretation. Such questions as "Why do you think so?" or "What is the author trying to say?" or "What would you have done if you had been the character?" will encourage everyone to give a personal interpretation of what was seen or heard.

Even if your child has little to share, she will still benefit from hearing other family members tell what a story means to them and explain or defend their statements. This exposure will help her become more conscious of how others think—which, in turn, will help her become more aware of her own higher-level thinking processes.

SUGGESTION: **Provide your youngster with reading material that encourages interpretation.**

The kinds of responses youngsters make to literature reflect their stages of intellectual development. Six- to eleven-year-old children, when asked to comment on what they have read, tend to respond with statements about the literal information presented in stories. Children in the twelve to sixteen age group often make statements that reveal that they are going beyond the actual words in a story to interpret. Interpretive response is not solely a product of a youngster's development, however; it is a product, also, of the kinds of writing she experiences.

In doing research in this area I noticed that after reading a story from a school text—a story that was highly explicit—only 7 percent of the statements a ten-year-old later made about the story were interpretive statements. Following the reading of a fairy tale in which little detail was presented, over 40 percent of her statements were interpretive. Though none of the information she gave appeared in the text, and no illustrations accompanied the story, the child gave a detailed description of what the hero looked like, what he wore, how he acted, what he was thinking, and what he intended to do.

When every thought, feeling, and deed is spelled out—as it so often is in children's books—youngsters have no need to use higher-level thinking. Only when there is something left for the reader to supply will youngsters have the opportunity to read and think interpretively. Folklore and contemporary stories and novels based on folkloric and archetypal themes, such as *The Hobbit* by J. R. R. Tolkien, tend to encourage interpretation because they are generally less dominated by literal information. For a listing of tales to interpret refer to the Suggested Reading section at the end of Part Three.

The mystery story, which has widespread appeal to youngsters in this age range, is a form of literature that will encourage your youngster to come up with her own interpretation of the information given in the text. When a youngster reads a Sherlock Holmes adventure, or even a Nancy Drew mystery, she is constantly making inferences about the available information in an attempt to beat the author to the solution of the mystery. In the process, though they are often unaware of it, youngsters review information and make predictions based on their own knowledge of both real life and fictional situations. They are involved in interpreting what they read.

It doesn't matter at what stage of reading development your youngster is, you can always find a mystery that will suit her.

SUGGESTION: Urge your youngster to use books as a source of dramatic scripts.

There is nothing most adolescent and preadolescent youngsters love more than an audience—particularly if that audience is a caring and appreciative family. You can capitalize on your child's showmanship and stimulate both her reading and interpretive thinking by suggesting that she put a well-liked book or short story into play form and produce it for a home audience. In adapting a story or novel, she will soon discover the importance of the author's use of description. Not only will she have to consider details of setting and characterization in reproducing a scene, she will have to consider each character's point of view.

To get this activity going, you might want to suggest that your youngster provide the Christmas holiday entertainment with a presentation of her own adaptation of Truman Capote's *Christmas Memories,* or entertain the gang on Halloween with a dramatic presentation of a Ray Bradbury or Edgar Allen Poe story.

If you have a video camera, use it to film the drama. If your daughter responds to the idea of making original films, follow up by suggesting that she use the text of a real play for the next production. Again, the process of reducing a play sufficiently to make it manageable for home film production will require serious interpretive efforts.

Under your guidance, your child's home experiences will have convinced her that access to written materials can provide something she wants. Now you need to keep that conviction alive by making certain she has an unending supply of adult literature.

Working with your child as she develops into a mature and avid reader will do wonders not only for her reading competence and confidence but for her self-esteem as well. It will also produce a dividend of incalculable worth: proof to your child that you respect and love her.

This idea brings us full circle.

The greatest gift you could give your child was the assurance of your love. The second greatest gift you could give was a set of tools with which to deal with life. A profound connection exists between these two gifts.

There is no greater assurance of one's love for another person than the willingness to devote quantities of time in that person's behalf.

To make your child a lifelong reader is to give him or her a perpetual reminder of your love, because a child who truly becomes a reader remains a reader through life.

Suggested Reading for Ages Twelve Through Sixteen

TEEN ROMANCE SERIES

Wildfire Romances, New York: Scholastic Inc.

Wishing Star Book, New York: Scholastic Inc.

Windswept Romances, New York: Scholastic Inc.

First Love, New York: Silhouette Books.

Sweet Dreams, New York: Bantam.

Young Love, New York: Dell.

Caprice Romances, New York: Putnam Publishing Group.

Juniper Books, New York: Fawcett Books.

YOUNG ADULT PROBLEM NOVELS
Guidelines for Choosing Young Adult Problem Novels

1. Look for stories that mirror your youngster's own developmental dilemmas.

2. Look for stories that focus upon a character with whom the reader can identify.

3. Look for stories that provide a solution to the reader's personal problems.

And Both Were Young, by Madeleine L'Engle. New York: Delacorte, 1983.

Ask Anybody, by Constance C. Greene. New York: Viking Press, 1983.

The Bigger Book of Lydia, by Margaret Wiley. New York: Harper and Row, 1983.

The Chocolate War, by Robert Cormier. New York: Pantheon Books, 1974.

Close to the Edge, by Gloria D. Miklowitz. New York: Delacorte, 1983.

Daphne's Book, by Mary Downing Hahn. New York: Clarion Books, 1983.

Dear Bill, Remember Me? and Other Stories, by Norma Mazer. New York: Delacorte, 1976.

Dinky Hocker Shoots Smack, by M. E. Kerr. New York: Harper and Row, 1972.

Forever, by Judy Blume. Scarsdale: Bradbury Press, 1975.

The Friends, by Rosa Guy. New York: Holt, Rinehart and Winston, 1973.

The Gift of Sarah Barker: a Novel, by Jane Yolen. New York: Viking Press, 1981.

Happily Ever After, by Judie Wolkoff. Scarsdale: Bradbury Press, 1981.

Hard Love, by Cynthia D. Grant. New York: Atheneum Publishing Co., 1983.

Hey, Didi Darling, by S. A. Kennedy. Boston: Houghton Mifflin Co., 1983.

Hideaway, by Eloise McGraw. New York: Atheneum Publishing Co., 1983.

Hold on to Love, by Mollie Hunter. New York: Harper and Row, 1984.

Hunter in the Dark, by Monica Hughes. New York: Atheneum Publishing Co., 1983.

In the Middle of a Rainbow, by Barbara Girion. New York: Charles Scribner's Sons, 1983.

It's Not What You Expect, by Norma Klein. New York: Avon Books, 1982.

Karen Kepplewhite is the World's Best Kisser, by Eve Bunting. New York: Clarion Books, 1983.

The Late Great Me, by Sandra Scoppetone. New York: Putnam Publishing Group, 1976.

Love in a Different Key, by Marjorie Franco. Boston: Houghton Mifflin Co., 1983.

Mom, the Wolf Man, and Me, by Norma Klein. New York: Avon Books, 1979.

No Safe Harbors, by Stephanie S. Tolan. New York: Charles Scribner's Sons, 1981.

The Redneck Poacher's Son, by Luke Wallin. Scarsdale: Bradbury Press, 1981.

The Scarecrows, by Robert Westall. New York: Greenwillow Books, 1981.

Slake's Limbo, by Felice Holman. New York: Charles Scribner's Sons, 1974.

Someone to Love, by Norma Fox Mazer. New York: Delacorte, 1983.

A Star for the Latecomer, by Bonnie Zindel and Paul Zindel. New York: Harper and Row, 1980.

A Summer to Die, by Lois Lowry. Boston: Houghton Mifflin Co., 1977.

That's Not My Style, by Mary Anderson. New York: Atheneum Publishing Co., 1983.

Then Again, Maybe I Won't, by Judy Blume. Scarsdale: Bradbury Press, 1971.

Underneath I'm Different, by Ellen Rabinowich. New York: Delacorte, 1983.

Walk Out a Brother, by Thomas Baird. New York: Harper and Row, 1983.

Who Loves Sam Grant? By Delores Beckman. New York: E. P. Dutton, 1983.

HEROES, HEROINES, AND THRILLS FOR YOUNG ADULTS

Guidelines for Choosing Books That Will Provide Outlets for Your Child's Fears and Impulses

1. Look for books whose central character is either involved in an activity your youngster is interested in, or is tackling a problem similar to one your youngster is wrestling with.

2. Look for books whose protagonists win acclaim for some quality of mind, body, or character.

3. Look for books that offer exciting reading.

The Black Pearl, by Scott O'Dell. New York: Dell Publishing Co., 1977.

The Blue Sword, by Robin McKinley. New York: Greenwillow Books, 1982.

Bridle the Wind, by Joan Aiken. New York: Delacorte, 1983.

Captains Courageous! by Rudyard Kipling. New York: Doubleday and Co., 1964.

The Clan of the Cave Bear, by Jean Auel. New York: Bantam Books, 1981.

The Deerslayer, by James Fenimore Cooper. New York: Charles Scribner's Sons, 1925.

Dragon of the Lost Sea, by Laurence Yep. New York: Harper and Row, 1982.

A Farewell to Arms, by Ernest Hemingway. New York: Charles Scribner's Sons, 1982.

Gabriel's Girl, by Norma Johnston. New York: Atheneum Publishing Co., 1983.

Hakon of Rogen's Saga, by Erik Haugaard. Boston: Houghton Mifflin Co., 1963.

Hew Against the Grain, by Betty S. Cummings. New York: Atheneum Publishing Co., 1977.

The Islanders, by John Rowe Townsend. Philadelphia: J. B. Lippincott, 1981.

Ivanhoe, by Sir Walter Scott. New York: Dodd, Mead and Co., 1983.

Jane Eyre, by Charlotte Brontë. New York: Bantam Books, 1981.

Johnny Tremain, by Esther Forbes. Boston: Houghton Mifflin Co., 1943.

Julie of the Wolves, by Jean C. George. New York: Harper and Row, 1972.

Kate and the Revolution, by John Rowe Townsend. Philadelphia: J. P. Lippincott, 1983.

Lord Jim, by Joseph Conrad. New York: Bantam Books, 1981.

Lords of the Triple Moons, by Ardath Mayhar. New York: Atheneum Publishing Co., 1983.

Mutiny on the Bounty, by Charles Nordhoff and James Norman Hall. Boston: Little, Brown and Co., 1932.

My Antonia, by Willa Cather. Boston: Little, Brown and Co., 1932.

National Velvet, by Enid Bagnold. New York: William Morrow and Co., 1949.

The Prince and the Pauper, by Mark Twain. Berkeley: University of California Press, 1983.

Prince of the Godborn, by Geraldine Harris. New York: Greenwillow Books, 1982.

Razor Eyes, by Richard Hough. New York: Lodestar Books, 1983.

The Red Badge of Courage, by Stephen Crane. New York: Scholastic, 1972.

The Scarlet Letter, by Nathaniel Hawthorne. New York: Airmont Publishing Co., 1964.

Shadrack's Crossing; a Novel by Avi. New York: Pantheon Books, 1983.

A Tale of Two Cities, by Charles Dickens. New York: Airmont Publishing Co., 1964.

Ware Hawk, by Andre Norton. New York: Atheneum Publishing Co., 1983.

Wuthering Heights, by Emily Brontë. New York: Dell Publishing Co., 1961.

Young Legionary, by Douglas Hill. New York: Atheneum Publishing Co., 1983.

ISSUE-ORIENTED READING *for* YOUNG ADULTS
Guidelines for Choosing Issue-Oriented Reading Material

1. Select books that deal with problems that concern your youngster.

2. Make sure the material is current.

3. Make sure the writing is interesting and lively.

All Times, All Peoples: A World History of Slavery, by Milton Meltzer. New York: Harper and Row, 1980.

The Animal Shelter, by Partricia Curtis. New York: Lodestar Books, 1984.

Anna to the Infinite Power, by Mildred Ames. New York: Scholastic, 1983.

The Autobiography of Miss Jane Pitman, by Ernest J. Gaines. New York: Dial Press, 1971.

Bury My Heart at Wounded Knee: An Indian History of the American West, by Dee Brown. New York: Holt, Rinehart and Winston, 1971.

The Chinese Americans, by Milton Meltzer. New York: Harper and Row, 1980.

Clone Catcher, by Alfred Stote. New York: Harper and Row, 1982.

Cloning and the New Genetics, by Margaret O. Hyde and Lawrence E. Hyde. Hillside: Enslow Publishers, 1984.

Feast or Famine? The Energy Future, by Franklin M. Branley. New York: Harper and Row, 1980.

Forecast 2000, by George Gallup, Jr., with William Proctor. New York: William Morrow and Co., 1984.

The Genetics Explosion, by Alvin Silverstein and Virginia Silverstein. Bristol: Four Winds Press, 1979.

The Girl on the Outside, by Mildred Pitts Walter. New York: Lothrop, Lee and Shepard Books, 1982.

Go Ask Alice (anonymous). Englewood Cliffs: Prentice-Hall, 1971.

God's Radar, by Fran Arrick. Scarsdale: Bradbury Press, 1983.

A Hero Ain't Nothing but a Sandwich, by Alice Childress. New York: Avon Books, 1982.

I Know Why the Caged Bird Sings, by Maya Angelou. New York: Bantam Books, 1971.

Lives at Stake: the Science and Politics of Environmental Health, by Laurence Pringle. New York: Macmillan Publishing Co., 1980.

Mischling, Second Degree: My Childhood in Nazi Germany, by Ilse Koehn. New York: Greenwillow Books, 1977.

My Brother Sam is Dead, by James L. Collier and Christopher Collier. Bristol: Four Winds Press, 1974.

The Nuclear Arms Race, by Ann E. Weiss. Boston: Houghton Mifflin Co., 1983.

Rescued! America's Endangered Wildlife on the Comeback Trail, by Olive W. Burt. New York: Julian Messner, 1980.

Sadako and the Thousand Paper Cranes, by Eleanor B. Coerr. New York: Putnam Publishing Group, 1977.

South Africa: Coming of Age under Apartheid, by Jason Laure and Ettagale Laure. New York: Farrar, Straus and Giroux, 1980.

Space Challenger: The Story of Guion Bluford, by Jim Haskins and Kathleen Benson. Minneapolis: Carolrhoda Books, 1984.

Space Ships of the Mind, by Nigel Calder. New York: Viking Press, 1978.

Tunnel Vision, by Fran Arrick. Scarsdale: Bradbury Press, 1980.

TALES TO INTERPRET

Guidelines for Choosing Thought-Provoking Literature

1. Look for writing that requires the reader to infer a character's thoughts, feelings, and intentions.

2. Look for writing that is metaphoric or that hides social truths in humor and satire.

3. Look for writing that stimulates the reader's imagination.

Across Five Aprils, by Irene Hunt. New York: Ace Books, 1982.

Annerton Pit, by Peter Dickinson. Boston: Little, Brown and Co., 1975.

Antigone, by Jean Anouilh. New York: French and European Publications, 1975.

Beauty: A Retelling of the Story of Beauty and the Beast, by Robin McKinley. New York: Harper and Row, 1978.

Big Red, by Jim Kjelgaard. New York: Holiday House, 1956.

The Catcher in the Rye, by J. D. Salinger. Boston: Little, Brown and Co., 1951.

The Cay, by Theodore Taylor. New York: Avon Books, 1970.

Ceremony of Innocence, by James Forman. New York: Hawthorne Books, 1970.

Chase Me, Catch Nobody, by Erik Haugaard. Boston: Houghton Mifflin Co., 1970.

Collision Course, by Nigel Hinton. New York: Lodestar Books, 1977.

Country of Broken Stone, by Nancy Bond. New York: Atheneum Publishing Co., 1979.

The Crucible, by Arthur Miller, in *Collected Plays.* New York: Penguin Books, 1976.

Dance of the Tiger, by Bjorn Kurten. New York: Pantheon Books, 1980.

The Dark Is Rising, by Susan Cooper. New York: Atheneum Publishing Co., 1973.

Daughter of Time, by Josephine Tey. Cutchogue: Buccaneer Books, 1951.

A Day No Pigs Would Die, by Robert Newton Peck. New York: Alfred A. Knopf, 1972.

The Diary of a Young Girl, by Anne Frank. New York: Doubleday, 1952.

Dicey's Song, by Cynthia Voight. New York: Atheneum Publishing Co., 1982.

Down the Long Hills, by Louis L'Amour. New York: Bantam Books, 1978.

Dragon Wings, by Laurence Yep. New York: Harper and Row, 1975.

The Exeter Blitz, by David Rees. New York: Lodestar Books, 1980.

Exit from Home, by Anita Heyman. New York: Crown, 1977.

The Farthest Shore, by Ursula Le Guin. New York: Bantam Books, 1975.

Firewood, by Jill Paton Walsh. New York: Avon Books, 1972.

Gone with the Wind, by Margaret Mitchell. New York: Avon Books, 1974.

The Good Earth, by Pearl S. Buck. New York: Pocket Books, 1975.

The Grounding of Group 6, by Julian F. Thompson. New York: Avon Books, 1983.

The Hessian, by Howard Fast. New York: William Morrow and Co., 1972.

House of Stairs, by William Sleator. New York: E. P. Dutton, 1974.

I Am the Cheese, by Robert Cormier. New York: Pantheon Books, 1977.

I, Juan de Parejo, by Elizabeth Borten de Frevino. New York: Farrar, Straus and Giroux, 1930.

Jacob Have I Loved, by Katherine Paterson. New York: Avon Books, 1981.

The King's Fifth, by Scott O'Dell. Boston: Houghton Mifflin Co., 1966.

The Learning Tree, by Gordon Parks. New York: Harper and Row, 1963.

The Life and Death of Yellow Bird, by James Foreman. New York: Farrar, Straus and Giroux, 1973.

The Light of the Forest, by Conrad Richter. New York: Alfred A. Knopf, 1953.

The Little Prince, by Antoine de Saint-Exupéry. New York: Harcourt Brace Jovanovich, 1968.

Little Women, by Louisa M. Alcott. New York: Macmillan Publishing Co., 1962.

Lord of the Flies, by William Golding. New York: Putnam Publishing Group, 1978.

Lord of the Rings, by J. R. R. Tolkien. Boston: Houghton Mifflin Co., 1974.

The Magical Adventures of Pretty Pearl, by Virginia Hamilton. New York: Harper and Row, 1983.

The Nick Adams Stories, by Ernest Hemingway. New York: Charles Scribner's Sons, 1981.

The Old Man and the Sea, by Ernest Hemingway. New York: Charles Scribner's Sons, 1952.

Old Yeller, by Fred Gipson. New York: Harper and Row, 1964.

The Once and Future King, by Terence White. New York: Putnam Publishing Group, 1958.

Path of the Pale Horse, by Paul Fleischman. New York: Harper and Row, 1983.

Rebecca, by Daphne Du Maurier. New York: Doubleday, 1938.

A Ring of Endless Light, by Madeleine L'Engle. New York: Farrar, Straus and Giroux, 1979.

Saint Joan, by George B. Shaw. New York: Penguin Books, 1958.

Sara Bishop, by Scott O'Dell. Boston: Houghton Mifflin Co., 1979.

Seaward, by Susan Cooper. New York: Atheneum Publishing Co., 1983.

The Shadow Guests, by Joan Aiken. New York: Delacorte, 1980.

The Snow Goose, by Paul Gallico. New York: Alfred A. Knopf, 1941.

A Storm in the Rain, by Jan Adkins. Boston: Little, Brown and Co., 1983.

A String in the Harp, by Nancy Bond. New York: Atheneum Publishing Co., 1976.

Sweet Whispers, Brother Rush, by Virginia Hamilton. New York: Putnam Publishing Group, 1982.

To Kill a Mockingbird, by Harper Lee. Philadelphia: J. P. Lippincott, 1960.

West Side Story, by Irving Shulman. New York: Pocket Books, 1961.

The Witch of Blackbird Pond, by Elizabeth George Speare. Boston: Houghton Mifflin Co., 1958.

The Yearling, by Marjorie Kinnan Rawlings. New York: Charles Scribner's Sons, 1982.

The Young Unicorns, by Madeleine L'Engle. New York: Farrar, Straus and Giroux, 1968.

Z for Zacharia, by Robert O'Brian. New York: Atheneum Publishing Co., 1975.

STORIES FOR FAMILY READING SESSIONS

Guidelines for Choosing Stories for Family Reading

1. Make sure the material is intellectually stimulating to the oldest child in the listening group.

2. Look for stories that are rich in language.

3. Look for stories that are strong in characterization.

4. Look for stories that provide emotional and intellectual impact.

5. Look for stories that raise questions.

"The Anarchists' Convention," by John Sayles. In *The Anarchists' Convention and Other Stories by John Sayles.* New York: Pocket Books, 1979.

And Then There Were None, by Agatha Christie. New York: Pocket Books, 1982.

"Battle Royal," by Ralph Ellison. In *Invisible Man.* New York: Random House, 1952.

"The Black Prince," by Shirley Ann Grau. In *The Black Prince.* New York: Alfred A. Knopf, 1953.

The Cask of Amontillado, by Edgar Allen Poe. Mahwah: Troll Associates, 1982.

"The Catbird Seat," by James Thurber. In *The Thurber Carnival.* New York: Harper and Row, 1945.

A Christmas Carol, by Charles Dickens. Cutchogue: Buccaneer Books, 1981.

Christmas Memories, by Truman Capote. New York: Random House, 1966.

"The Diamond as Big as the Ritz," by F. Scott Fitzgerald. In *Babylon Revisited and Other Stories,* by F. Scott Fitzgerald. New York: Charles Scribner's Sons, 1971.

"For Esme with Love and Squalor," by J. D. Salinger. In *Nine Stories by J. D. Salinger.* Boston: Little, Brown and Co., 1950.

The Gift of the Magi, by O. Henry. Mankato: Creative Education, 1980.

The Halloween Tree, by Ray Bradbury. New York: Bantam Books, 1982.

The Law of Life, by Jack London. Providence: Jamestown, 1976.

"The Lottery," by Shirley Jackson. In *The Lottery.* New York: Farrar, Straus and Giroux, 1949.

"The Magic Barrel," by Bernard Malamud. In *The Magic Barrel.* New York: Farrar, Straus and Giroux, 1958.

No Room in the Ark, by Alan Moorehead. New York: Harper and Row, 1960.

"The Pearl," by John Steinbeck. In *The Short Novels of John Steinbeck*. New York: Viking Press, 1963.

"The Rocking Horse Winner," by D. H. Lawrence. In *The Complete Stories of D. H. Lawrence*, volume 3. New York: Viking Press, 1933.

"The Snows of Kilimanjaro," by Ernest Hemingway. In *The Snows of Kilimanjaro and Other Stories*. New York: Charles Scribner's Sons, 1982.

The Son of the Wolf, by Jack London. Oakland: Star Rover House, 1980.

"A Sunset on the Veld," by Doris Lessing. In *African Stories*. New York: Simon and Schuster, 1965.

Short Story Collections:

Alfred Hitchcock's Tales to Fill You with Fear and Trembling, edited by Eleanor Sullivan. New York: Dial Press, 1980.

The Androids Are Coming: Seven Stories of Science Fiction, edited by Robert Silverberg. New York: Lodestar Books, 1979.

The Call of the Wild, White Fang, and Other Stories, edited by Andrew Sinclair. New York: Penguin Books, 1981.

The Door in the Hedge, by Robin McKinley. New York: Greenwillow Books, 1981.

Eight Plus One, by Robert Cormier. New York: Pantheon Books, 1980.

Tales out of Time, compiled and edited by Barbara Ireson. New York: Putnam Publishing Group, 1981.

Tantalizing Locked Room Mysteries, edited by Martin Greenberg and Charles Waugh. New York: Walker and Co., 1982.

Those Amazing Electronic Thinking Machines, edited by Isaac Asimov, Martin Greenberg and Charles Waugh. New York: Franklin Watts, 1983.

The titles of additional books with carefully selected recommended reading lists may be found in the Appendix.

MAGAZINES *FOR* AGES TWELVE *TO* SIXTEEN

Boy's Life, 1325 Walnut Hill Lane, Irving, TX, 75062.

Nautica, Pickering Wharf, Salem, MA, 01970.

National Geographic, 17 and M Streets, N. W., Washington, D. C., 20036.

Hot Rod, 8490 Sunset Blvd., Los Angeles, CA, 90069.

Surfer, Box 1028, Dana Point, CA, 92629.

Tiger Beat, 105 Union Avenue, Cresskill, NJ, 07626.

3-2-1 Contact, One Lincoln Plaza, New York, NY, 10023.

Appendix

Learning to Read, by Bruno Bettelheim, and Zelan, Karen. New York: Random House, 1983. Titles for all ages.

Junior High School Library Catalog, edited by Gary C. Bogart and Richard H. Isaacson. New York: H. W. Wilson & Co., 1980. Titles for mid teens.

Babies Need Books, by Dorothy Butler. New York: Atheneum, 1980. Titles for ages 1-5.

Books and the Teenage Reader: A Guide for Teachers, Librarians, and Parents, by Robert G. Carlsen. New York: Harper and Row, 1980.

Good Books to Grow On, by Andrea E. Cascardi. New York: Warner Books, 1985. Titles for all ages.

The Bookfinder—A Guide to Children's Literature, an annual library sourcebook by Sharon Spredemann Dreyer. Circle Pines, MN: American Guidance Service. Titles for ages 2-15.

How to Choose Good Books for Your Children, by Kate Hall-McMullan. Boston: Addison-Wesley, 1984. Titles for all ages.

Choosing Books for Children, by Betsy Hearne. New York: Delacorte, 1982. Titles for infants to teenagers.

for Reading Out Loud!, by Margaret M. Kimmel and Elizabeth Segal. New York: Delacorte, 1983. Titles for ages 2-15.

A Parent's Guide to Children's Reading, by Nancy Larrick. New York: Bantam, 1982. Titles for all ages.

Learning to Read, by Margaret Meek. Salem: Bodley Head, 1982. Titles for ages 2-15.

Read Aloud, by Jim Trelease. New York: Penguin Books, 1985. Titles for all ages.

Bibliography

Applebee, Arthur N. "The Spectator Role: Theoretical and Developmental Studies of Ideas About and Responses to Literature, with Special Reference to Four Age Levels." Ph.D. dissertation, University of London. ERIC document ED 114 840.

_____. "The Elements of Response to a Literary Work: What We Have Learned." *Research in the Teaching of English,* Winter 1977, pp. 255–271. ERIC/RCS Report.

_____. *The Child's Concept of Story.* Chicago: University of Chicago Press, 1978.

Allington, Richard L., and McGill-Franzen, Anne. "Word Identification Errors in Isolation and in Context: Apples vs. Oranges." *The Reading Teacher* 33 (1980):795–800.

Asher, S. R. "Influence of Topic Interest on Black Children's and White Children's Reading Comprehension." *Child Development* 50 (1979):686–690.

Asher, S. R.; Hymel, S.; and Wigfield, A. "Influence of Topic Interest on Children's Reading Comprehension." *Journal of Reading Behavior* 10 (1978):35–47.

Ashton-Warner, Sylvia. *Teacher.* New York: Bantam, 1963.

Bettelheim, Bruno. *The Uses of Enchantment.* New York: Vintage Books, 1977.

Bower, Gordon H., and Gilligan, Stephen G. "Remembering Information Related to One's Self." *Journal of Research in Personality* 13 (1979):420–430.

Bransford, J. D.; Barclay, J. R.; and Franks, J. J. "Sentence Memory: A Constructive Versus Interpretive Approach." *Cognitive Psychology* 3 (1972):193–209.

Bransford, J. D.; and Johnson, M. K. "Contextual Prerequisites for Understanding: Some Investigations of Comprehension and Recall." *Journal of Verbal Learning and Verbal Behavior* 11 (1972):717–726.

Breen, M. J. "The Survey of School Attitudes: An Elementary Grade Attitudinal Survey." *The Wisconsin Counselor* 1 (1977):28–30.

Britton, James N. *Language and Learning.* London: The Penguin Press, 1970.

Brookover, Wilbur B.; LePere, Jean M.; Hamachek, Don E.; Shailer, Thomas; and Erickson, Edsel L. "Improving Academic Achievement through Students' Self-Concept Enhancement." *Self Concept of Ability and Scholastic*

Achievement, Final Report on Cooperative Research Project No. 1636, October 1965.

Brookover, Wilbur B.; Paterson, Ann; and Shailer, Thomas. "The Relationship of Self-Image to Achievement in Junior High School Subjects." *Self Concept of Ability and School Achievement,* Cooperative Research Project No. 845, December 1962.

Brown, James I., and McDowell, Earl E. "The Role of Self-Image on Reading Rate and Comprehension Achievement." *Reading Improvement* 16 (1970):22–27.

Brzeinski, E. J., and Elledge, G. "What Strategies Are Best in Preschool Beginning Reading Programs?" In *Some Persistent Questions on Beginning Reading.* Edited by R. Aukerman. Newark, Delaware: International Reading Association, 1972.

Carlsen, G. Robert. *Books and the Teenage Reader: A Guide for Teacher, Librarians, and Parents.* New York: Harper and Row, 1980.

Carroll, John B. "Psycholinguistics and the Study and Teaching of Reading." In *Aspects of Reading Education.* Edited by Susanna Pflaum-Connor. Berkeley, CA: McCutchan Publishing Corp., 1978.

Clark, Margaret M. *Young Fluent Readers.* London: Heinemann Educational Books, 1976.

Cohen, Rachel. *L'Apprentissage Precose de la Lecture.* Paris: Presses Universitaires de France, 1977.

Crist, Robert L., and Petrone, Joseph M. "Learning Concepts from Contexts and Definitions." *Journal of Reading Behavior* 9 (1977):301–303.

Doman, G. *Teach Your Baby to Read.* New York: Random House, 1963.

Durkin, Dolores. "Earlier Start in Reading?" *Elementary School Journal* 63 (1962):146–159.

———. *Teaching Young Children to Read.* Boston: Allen and Bacon, 1980.

———. "A Fifth Year Report on the Achievement of Early Readers." *Elementary School Journal* 65, no. 2 (1964):76–80.

———. "Early Readers: Reflections After Six Years of Research." *The Reading Teacher* 18 (1964):3–7.

———. *Children Who Read Early.* New York: Teachers College Press, Columbia University, 1966.

———. *When Should Children Begin to Read?* 67th Yearbook of the National Society for the Study of Education, Part II. Chicago: University of Chicago Press, 1968.

———. "A Language Arts Program for Pre-First Grade Children: Two-Year Achievement Report." *Reading Research Quarterly* 5, no. 4 (1970): 524–533.

Favat, F. Andre. *Child and Tale: The Origins of Interest.* Research Report No. 19, National Council of Teachers of English. Urbana, 1977.

Flapan, Dorothy. *Children's Understanding of Social Interaction.* New York: Teachers College Press, 1968.

Franks, J. J., and Bransford, J. D. "The Acquisition of Abstract Ideas." *Journal of Verbal Learning* 11 (1972):311–315.

Freud, Sigmund. *Character and Culture.* New York: Colliers Books, MacMillan Publishing Co., Inc., 1963.

Gibson, Eleanor J., and Levin, Harry. *The Psychology of Reading.* Cambridge, Mass.: The MIT Press, 1975.

Ginott, Haim G. *Between Parent and Child.* New York: MacMillan, 1965.

Gipe, Joan P. "Use of a Relevant Context Helps Kids Learn New Word Meanings." *The Reading Teacher* 33 (1980):398–402.

Goodman, K. S. "A Linguistic Study of Cues and Miscues in Reading." *Elementary English* 42 (1965):639–743.

———. "Reading: A Psycholinguistic Guessing Game." *Journal of the Reading Specialist* 6 (1967):126–135.

Harding, D. W. "The Role of the Onlooker." *Scrutiny* 6, no. 3 (1937).

———. "Psychological Processes in the Reading of Fiction." *British Journal of Aesthetics* 2 (1962):133–147.

Holland, Norman. *The Dynamics of Literary Response.* New York: Oxford University Press, 1968.

Inhelder, B., and Piaget, J. *The Early Growth of Logic in the Child.* New York: Norton, 1964.

Kimmel, Margaret Mary, and Segel, Elizabeth. *For Reading Out Loud!* New York: Dell Publishing Co., 1984.

Kohlberg, L. "Early Education: A Cognitive-Developmental View." *Child Development* 39, no. 4 (1968):1013–1062.

Kolers, Paul A. "Three Stages of Reading." In *Basic Studies on Reading.* Edited by H. Levin, and J. P. Williams. New York: Basic Books, Inc. 1970.

Lewis, J. "Do Children Really Learn to Dislike School?" Paper presented at the Wisconsin Educational Research Association Conference. Madison, February 1974.

Lewis, Shari. *Making Easy Puppets.* New York: E. P. Dutton, 1967.

Loban, Walter. *Language Development: Kindergarten through Grade Twelve.* Urbana: National Council of Teachers of English, 1976.

Menyuk, Paula. "The Acquisition and Development of Language." In *Current Research in Developmental Psychology Series.* Edited by John C. Wright. Englewood Cliffs, N.J.: Prentice Hall, 1971.

Miller, George A. *Spontaneous Apprentices: Children and Language.* New York: Seaburg, 1977.

Moore, O. K.; Burns, L.; Carpentier, J.; Jefferson, F.; Moore, R.; and Semero, S. "Academic Competence and Self-Esteem." An Evaluation of the Pittsburgh Clarifying Environments Projects in the Hall District. Pittsburgh, September, 1972.

Morphett, Mabel Vogel, and Washburne, Carleton. "When Should Children Begin to Read?" *Elementary School Journal* 31 (1931):496–503.

Perfetti, C. A. "Language Comprehension and Fast Decoding: Some Psycholinguistic Prerequisites for Skilled Reading Comprehension." Paper presented to the Development of Reading Comprehension Seminar of the International Reading Association. Newark, Delaware, July 1975.

Piaget, Jean. *The Language and Thought of the Child.* New York: Harcourt Brace, & World, 1926.

Pitcher, E. G., and Prelinger, E. *Children Tell Stories: An Analysis of Fantasy.* New York: International Universities Press, 1963.

Rayner, K., and Hagelberg, E. M. "Word Recognition Cues for Beginning and Skilled Readers." *Journal of Experimental Child Psychology* 20 (1975):444–455.

Shankweiler, D. E., and Liberman, I. Y. "Misreading: A Search for Causes." In *Language by Ear and by Eye.* Edited by J. F. Kavanagh, and I. G. Mattingly. Cambridge, Mass.: MIT Press, 1969.

Smith, Frank. *Essays Into Literacy.* London: Heinemann Educational Books, 1983.

Smith, H. K. "The Responses of Good and Poor Readers when Asked to Read for Different Purposes." *Reading Research Quarterly* 3 (1967):53–83.

Smith, Mary K. "Measurement of the Size of General English Vocabulary Through the Elementary Grades and High School." *Genetic Psychology Monographs* 24 (1941):311–345.

Sobkov, Jason, and Moody, Mark. "Memory and Reading: The Effects of Semantic Context on Word Identification." *The Journal of General Psychology* 100 (1979):229–236.

Soderbergh, Ragnhild. "Learning to Read between Two and Five: Some Observations on Normal Hearing and Deaf Children." Paper presented for the Georgetown University Round Table on Language and Linguistics. 1976.

———. *Reading in Early Childhood.* Washington: Georgetown University Press, 1977.

Spiro, Rand J.; Bruce, Bertram C.; and Brewer, William F. *Theoretical Issues in Reading Comprehension. Perspectives from Cognitive Psychology, Linguistics, Artificial Intelligence, and Education.* Hillsdale, N.J.: Lawrence Erlbaum Associates, Publishers, 1980.

Steinberg, Danny, and Steinberg, Miho. "Reading Before Speaking." *Visible Language* 9 (1975):197–224.

Urbana. University of Illinois. "Topic Interest, External Incentive and Reading Comprehension." [By Asher, S. R., and Geraci, R. L.]

U.S. Department of Health, Education, and Welfare, The National Institute of Education, *Becoming a Nation of Readers: The Report of the Commission on Reading,* prepared by Anderson, Richard C.; Hiebert, Elfrieda H.; Scott, Judith A.; and Wilkinson, Ian, A.G. (Washington, D.C.).

Weeks, Thelma E. "Early Reading Acquisition as Language Development." *Language Arts* 56, no. 5 (1979):515–520.

Index

About the Authors

Jacquelyn Gross, Ed.D., is an educator with teaching experience at elementary, junior high, high school, and university levels in the United States and France. She holds five California teaching and administrative credentials for both regular and special education, and has a master's degree in education with a specialty in reading. She has also taught Children's Literature at California State University, Dominguez Hills. She is currently completing a comprehensive computer program for the development of reading comprehension.

Leonard Gross is a journalist, novelist, and screenwriter, the winner of multiple awards and the author or co-author of many books on a wide variety of subjects.